THE  TIMES

MILLENNIUM
·
QUIZ BOOK

THE ⬥ TIMES
MILLENNIUM
QUIZ BOOK

Howard Robin

TIMES BOOKS
London

The Times Millennium Quiz Book
Published by
Times Books
HarperCollins*Publishers*
77-85 Fulham Palace Road
London W6 8JB

Printed and bound in Great Britain by Caledonian

British Library Cataloguing in Publication Data
A catalogue record for this book is available from
the British Library

ISBN 0 7230 1061 7

Contents

Introduction

The Times Millennium Quiz Book contains a challenging array of 2000 questions, drawn from the last 1000 years. The questions are arranged by century, starting with the 20th at the beginning of the book and finishing with the 11th at the end. Each century is divided into individual quizzes of 20 questions. The questions are on the right-hand page with the answers on the following left-hand page.

The quiz covers a wide range of subjects: not just history, but people, places, discoveries, science, the arts, sport, cinema and music, to name but some. With its span of 1000 years, *The Times Millennium Quiz Book* has been designed to offer a tantalising and stimulating voyage through ten centuries of change.

Howard Robin

1 What are the names of the two rival pigs in *Animal Farm*?

2 Which Free City was annexed by Germany at the beginning of the Second World War?

3 In which year did a British player last win the men's singles final at Wimbledon?

4 Which Beatle is in the lead as they cross the road on the cover of their *Abbey Road* album?

5 What is the name of Rick's love rival in *Casablanca*?

6 Which two ships led the taskforce sent to recapture the Falklands?

7 Who shared the 1962 Nobel Prize for Physiology or Medicine for work on the molecular structure of DNA?

8 What species of parrot does Michael Palin sell to John Cleese in Monty Python's Dead Parrot Sketch?

9 Which were Margaret Thatcher's two 'flagship' Tory councils?

10 Which English footballers missed in the 1990 World Cup semi-final penalty shoot-out won by Germany?

11 Why did Dylan Thomas choose the name Llaregub for his fictional village in *Under Milk Wood*?

12 Where are the headquarters of CNN?

13 What was the nickname of the Model T Ford?

14 Who was the 20th century's longest ruling dictator?

15 Which iconic peer drowned when the cruiser *Hampshire* struck an enemy mine in 1916?

16 What does the acronym LASER stand for?

17 When was the Winter of Discontent in which industrial chaos swept Britain?

18 What is the cruising speed of Concorde?

19 What name is given to Lloyd George's Budget of 1909 which was rejected by the House of Lords?

20 Who played the Pinball Wizard in the film *Tommy*?

1   Napoleon and Snowball

2   Danzig (Gdansk) in Poland

3   1936, when Fred Perry won

4   John Lennon

5   Victor Laszlo

6   HMS Hermes and Invincible

7   James Dewey Watson, Francis Crick and Maurice Wilkins

8   Norwegian Blue

9   Wandsworth and Westminster

10   Stuart Pearce and Chris Waddle

11   For its meaning when spelt backwards

12   Atlanta, Georgia

13   Tin Lizzie

14   Kim Il Sung, leader of North Korea from 1948 until 1994

15   Lord Kitchener

16   Light amplification by stimulated emission of radiation

17   1978-9

18   Mach 2 or twice the speed of sound

19   People's Budget

20   Elton John

1   Which 1991 movie is subtitled *Judgement Day*?

2   Which Nazi leader was imprisoned in the Tower of London?

3   Which writer was dubbed 'the bard of mean streets'?

4   What was Elvis Presley's first number 1 record?

5   Where and when was the first atomic bomb exploded?

6   What are the three theatres in the Royal National Theatre building?

7   Who was England's goalkeeper when Maradona scored the Hand of God goal in 1986?

8   Who led the Liberals to an overwhelming electoral victory in 1906?

9   What was the name of the King's Road shop run by Malcolm McLaren and Vivienne Westwood?

10 Who was US president when NATO was created?

11 What was the title of the Debussy-scored ballet by Nijinsky in which he played a faun among nymphs in a field?

12 What was the first effective treatment for TB?

13 Which Evelyn Waugh novel is subtitled: The Sacred and Profane Memories of Captain Charles Ryder?

14 Which countries signed the Warsaw Pact?

15 Where were the two simultaneous Live Aid concerts held in 1985?

16 What major change was made to the Bank of England in 1946?

17 Which arts movement was launched as 'pure psychic automatism' by poet Andre Breton in the '20s?

18 What was the name of Sir Malcolm Campbell's speedboat and car in which he set land-speed and water-speed records?

19 Who was the heartless tramp played by Marlene Dietrich in *The Blue Angel*?

20 Which philosopher wrote *Sein und Seit* (*Being and Time*)?

20th Century

1   Terminator 2

2   *Rudolf Hess*

3   *Detective writer Raymond Chandler*

4   Heartbreak Hotel

5   *Alamogordo, New Mexico in the Trinity Test of July 1945*

6   *Olivier, Lyttelton and Cottesloe*

7   *Peter Shilton*

8   *Henry Campbell-Bannerman*

9   Sex

10 *President Truman (1949)*

11 L'Après Midi d'un Faune

12 *Streptomycin, discovered in 1944*

13 Brideshead Revisited

14 *Albania, Bulgaria, Czechoslovakia, German Democratic Republic, Hungary, Poland, Romania, Soviet Union*

15 *London and Philadelphia*

16 *It was nationalised*

17 *Surrealism*

18 Bluebird

19 *Lola*

20 *Martin Heidegger*

1 Who came second to Margaret Thatcher in the 1975 ballot that ousted Edward Heath as Tory leader?

2 What are the names of the five members of TV's Simpson family?

3 Which new state was proclaimed at the Gate of Heavenly Peace on 1 October 1949?

4 What was the Rolling Stones' last UK number 1 single, in 1969?

5 Which chancellor introduced old age pensions to Britain?

6 Which was the first football team from outside the British Isles to beat England at Wembley?

7 Who discovered that the universe was expanding?

8 Who plays the part of the scientist Claude Lacombe in *Close Encounters of the Third Kind*?

9 What is the full name of the drug LSD?

10 Which former prisoner of the Nazis became the first chancellor of West Germany?

11 What were car-makers Rolls and Royce's first names?

12 Who played the parts of lawman Will Kane and his bride Amy in the film *High Noon*?

13 Which were the original six members of the Common Market?

14 What is the title of the completely silent work by avant garde composer John Cage?

15 Which general seized control of South Vietnam in 1963?

16 Of whom did the poet W.H. Auden write: 'All he did was to remember like the old and be honest like children'?

17 At which village was mustard gas first used in war?

18 Which European country has the world's highest population density?

19 What is the first name of the Great Gatsby in the novel by Scott Fitzgerald?

20 What does the medical term ECT stand for?

1   William Whitelaw

2   Marge, Homer, Lisa, Bart, Maggie

3   The Communist Republic of China, by Mao Tse-tung

4   Honky Tonk Women, 1969

5   Lloyd George

6   Hungary, who won 6-3 in 1953

7   Edwin Hubble

8   Film director François Truffaut

9   Lysergic Acid Diethylamide

10   Konrad Adenauer

11   Charles Stewart Rolls and Frederick Henry Royce

12   Gary Cooper and Grace Kelly

13   France, Germany, Italy, Belgium, Netherlands and Luxembourg

14   4 minutes and 33 seconds

15   Nguyen Van Thieu

16   Sigmund Freud – In Memory of Sigmund Freud

17   Passchendaele, 1917, in the third battle of Ypres

18   Monaco, 32,097 per square kilometre

19   Jay

20   Electroconvulsive therapy

20th Century

1   Who was born at 17 Bruton Street?

2   Who said: 'How can you govern a country which produces 246 kinds of cheese?'

3   Which major sporting event was declared void in April 1993?

4   What was the month and year of John Lennon's murder?

5   Which 15-minute piece of music consisting of a relentless rhythm under a repetitive theme was a sensation at its Paris debut in the '20s?

6   Who was Secretary-General of the United Nations when the People's Republic of China was admitted?

7   What was Hitler's star sign?

8   What are the six counties of Northern Ireland?

9   Which American writer used the fictional location Yoknapatawpha in many of his books?

10   What was the name of Andy Warhol's studio?

11   Which minister of health created the National Health Service?

12   Where is Britain's Chemical and Biological Defence Establishment?

13   Which doctor creates the monster Rocky in *The Rocky Horror Show*?

14   Which discovery did Otto Hahn and Fritz Strassmann make in 1939?

15   Who was the founding father of Pakistan and its first Governor-General?

16   Which company launched the drug Valium in 1963?

17   Which actor has played the most leading roles in films?

18   In which decade were the first 'Spock' babies born?

19   Who said: 'The Suez Canal is flowing through my drawing room'?

20   What was the name of the spacecraft – which is the Russian word for 'east' – in which Yuri Gagarin became the first man to be launched into space?

1   The Queen

2   French president Charles de Gaulle

3   The Grand National, after demonstrators ran onto the course and a false start

4   December 1980

5   Ravel's Bolero

6   U Thant, in 1971

7   Cusp of Aries and Taurus

8   Antrim, Armagh, Down, Fermanagh, Derry and Tyrone

9   William Faulkner

10   The Factory

11   Aneurin Bevan

12   Porton Down, Wiltshire

13   Dr Frank N. Furter

14   Nuclear fission

15   Muhammad Ali Jinnah

16   Roche Laboratories

17   John Wayne – 153

18   The 1940s, following publication of Dr Benjamin Spock's Common Sense Book of Baby and Child Care, in 1946

19   Lady Eden, wife of prime minister Sir Anthony Eden during the Suez crisis of 1956

20   Vostok, in 1961

1 What is the name of the country of which Groucho Marx is dictator in *Duck Soup*?

2 Which was the only joint action – in 1968 – in which armies of the Warsaw Pact countries collaborated?

3 Who were the three astronauts on the *Apollo 11* mission that put the first men on the moon?

4 What did the periods 1928-32, 1933-7 and 1938-42 have in common in the history of Communism?

5 Which was the first single by the Sex Pistols?

6 What did the United States spend $17,000 million on in Europe between 1948 and 1952?

7 Who writes the *Harry Potter* books?

8 What are the ingredients of a Margarita cocktail?

9 Who was Churchill's minister of labour during the war?

10 What was found in the Valley of the Kings, near Luxor?

11 What is Madonna's surname?

12 In which film does Charlie Chaplin eat his boot and laces?

13 Which English poet wrote: 'Give me your arm, old toad; Help me down Cemetery Road.'

14 What was the name of the Russian dog that became the first living creature to orbit the Earth?

15 Which European leader ruled his country from 1946 until 1985?

16 Who first used the F-word on British TV?

17 Which was the first Carry On film?

18 Who was the US President at the time of the Wall Street Crash?

19 At what level was Britain's minimum wage set in 1999?

20 Who was the first Footballer of the Year?

1 *Freedonia*

2 *The invasion of Czechoslovakia*

3 *Mike Collins, Neil Armstrong and Edwin 'Buzz' Aldrin, in 1969*

4 *They all marked Five-Year Plans by Stalin to restructure the Soviet economy*

5 Anarchy in the UK

6 *The Marshall Plan, or European Recovery Programme, initiated after World War II*

7 *J.K. Rowling*

8 *Tequila, Cointreau, lemon, lime, ice and salt*

9 *Ernest Bevin*

10 *The tomb of Tutankhamun*

11 *Ciccone*

12 The Goldrush

13 *Philip Larkin*

14 *Laika*

15 *Enver Hoxha of Albania*

16 Kenneth Tynan

17 Carry On Sergeant

18 Herbert Hoover

19 *£3.60 an hour*

20 *Stanley Matthews, in 1948*

1 What was the month and year of the Queen's coronation?

2 What did the city of Stalingrad change its name to in 1961?

3 What make of guitar did Jimi Hendrix play?

4 Whose Quantum Theory revolutionised modern physics?

5 Which opera features an American naval officer named Pinkerton?

6 Which five territories did Israel capture during the Six-Day War of 1967?

7 Who retired with an estimated $500 million fortune in 1901 – and then gave much of it away?

8 Which was the first British football team to win the European Cup?

9 Who came second and third behind Bill Clinton in the 1992 presidential election?

10 Which two momentous events took place in a railway carriage at Compiègne?

11 What do the initials DNA stand for?

12 What came to an end at the battle of Dien Bien Phu in 1954?

13 To the nearest five billion pounds, how much is Bill Gates worth?

14 What name is given to the frontier line between Poland and Germany laid down at the end of the Second World War?

15 Which song contains the line: 'Take your protein pills and put your helmet on'?

16 What does the abbreviation PVC stand for?

17 What was dictator General Franco's title?

18 What was the highest civilian honour of the Soviet Union?

19 Upon which story by Joseph Conrad is the classic Hollywood war film *Apocalypse Now* based?

20 Over which issue was a referendum held in Britain in 1979?

1   *June 1953*

2   *Volgograd*

3   *Fender Stratocaster*

4   *Max Planck's*

5   Madam Butterfly

6   *Sinai Peninsula, Gaza Strip, West Bank of the Jordan, East Jerusalem and Golan Heights*

7   *Industrialist and philanthropist Andrew Carnegie*

8   *Glasgow Celtic, in 1967*

9   *George Bush and Ross Perot*

10   *The formal surrender of Germany to the Allies in 1918 and the French surrender to Germany in 1940*

11   *Deoxyribonucleic acid*

12   *French rule in Indo-China*

13   *£56 billion, according to Forbes magazine in 1999*

14   *Oder-Neisse Line*

15   David Bowie's Space Oddity

16   *Polyvinyl chloride*

17   *Caudillo (leader)*

18   The Order of Lenin

19   Heart of Darkness

20   *Devolution*

1   What was unusual about the 1930 film *Anna Christie*?

2   Which were the only two occasions when Churchill, Roosevelt and Stalin met?

3   Where was Einstein working when he published his Special Theory of Relativity?

4   Who was the defendant in the Lady Chatterley trial?

5   What was the month and year of the assassination of President Kennedy?

6   In which order did England and Germany score the six goals of the 1966 World Cup final?

7   What is the name of the world champion whom Rocky defeats in the first Rocky film?

8   What is the English title of the novel *Der Zauberberg*?

9   Which was the first major rock event to raise money for charity?

10 On whose country estate did Christine Keeler and John Profumo first meet?

11 There are 43 trillion wrong ways to arrange what?

12 What is the name of the gangster union boss played by Lee J. Cobb in the film *On the Waterfront*?

13 In which two cities are Nobel Prizes presented?

14 Who first flew across the English Channel?

15 Who were the four members of the Beyond the Fringe team?

16 What is the title of Freud's book about dreams, published in 1900?

17 Who was Secretary-General of the United Nations at the time of the Suez Crisis?

18 Which US firm launched the Pentium 64-bit microprocessor?

19 Which two architects designed the Pompidou Centre?

20 What was hung upside down in the Piazzale Loreto in Milan in April 1945?

1   It was the first in which Greta Garbo spoke

2   The wartime summit conferences at Teheran (1943) and Yalta (1945)

3   In the Patent Office in Berne, Switzerland

4   Penguin Books, in 1960

5   November 1963

6   Germany/England/England/Germany/(extra time) England/England

7   Apollo Creed

8   The Magic Mountain, by Thomas Mann

9   The Concerts for Bangladesh at Madison Square Garden, 1971

10   Lord Astor's Cliveden estate

11   The Rubik cube

12   Johnny Friendly

13   The Peace Prize is presented in Oslo. The other prizes are presented in Stockholm

14   Louis Blériot, in 1909

15   Peter Cook, Dudley Moore, Jonathan Miller and Alan Bennet

16   The Interpretation of Dreams

17   Dag Hammarskjöld, in 1956

18   Intel

19   Richard Rogers and Renzo Piano

20   The corpse of Mussolini

1 Who sang *Tutti Frutti, Long Tall Sally* and *Good Golly Miss Molly*?

2 Which part of Czechoslovakia did Germany get under the Munich agreement?

3 What is the name of working-class Jimmy Porter's upper-class wife in *Look Back in Anger*?

4 Which Tsar was murdered with his family in a cellar at Ekaterinburg in 1918?

5 Which historic agreement did Britain and France sign on 8 April 1904?

6 What is the name of the fading actress played by Gloria Swanson in *Sunset Boulevard*?

7 What does 'Sinn Fein' mean?

8 For which life-saving discovery did Sir Frederick Banting and John Macleod win the 1923 Nobel Prize for medicine?

9 Which country was joined to Hungary from the 12th century until the beginning of the 20th?

10 What are the first names of the four members of ABBA?

11 What was the formal term for President Reagan's 'Star Wars' project?

12 Who starred in *The Sheikh* and *Blood and Sand*?

13 In which European country did the 'Revolution of Flowers' take place?

14 What does V/STOL stand for in aeronautics?

15 On which day and in which month did Al Capone's mobsters wipe out Bugs Moran's gang?

16 Who choreographed *West Side Story*?

17 Who led the Dambusters?

18 Who replaced Ayatollah Khomeini as president of Iran?

19 Who was the first director of the National Theatre?

20 Which are the six official working languages of the United Nations?

1 *Little Richard*

2 *Sudetenland*

3 *Alison*

4 *Tsar Nicholas II*

5 *The Entente Cordiale*

6 *Norma Desmond*

7 *Ourselves Alone*

8 *Insulin*

9 *Croatia*

10 *Agnetha, Bjorn, Benny, Anni-frid*

11 *Strategic Defence Initiative (SDI)*

12 *Rudolph Valentino*

13 *Portugal, in 1974*

14 *Vertical short take-off and landing*

15 *14 February, in the St. Valentine's Day Massacre of 1929*

16 *Jerome Robbins*

17 *Guy Gibson*

18 *Hojatoleslam Rafsanjani*

19 *Laurence Olivier*

20 *English, Chinese, Russian, French, Spanish and Arabic*

1 Who was British prime minister at the time of the General Strike?

2 The title of which novel about a group of American airmen has passed into the English language?

3 What was Mahatma Gandhi's first name?

4 Who directed the film *Battleship Potemkin*?

5 Which four leaders drew up the Munich Agreement?

6 Who founded Tamla Motown records?

7 For which theatre company did Chekhov write *The Cherry Orchard* and *The Three Sisters*?

8 How much did you get for thirteen shillings and sixpence after decimalization?

9 Which prime minister did the Bolsheviks oust when they seized power?

10 Who has won the most Best Actress Oscars?

11 Which three sovereign countries of Europe are not members of the United Nations?

12 Which three Brits have won the Wimbledon singles title since the war?

13 Which conference established the International Monetary Fund?

14 Who was George Gershwin's main lyricist?

15 Who became king after the abdication of Edward VIII?

16 Who was the first woman in space?

17 Near which river did the British and French halt the German advance on Paris in 1914?

18 Who directed *This is Spinal Tap*?

19 Who were the last three Poet Laureates of the 20th century?

20 To which leading Zionist was the Balfour Declaration of British support for a homeland in Palestine made?

1 *Stanley Baldwin, in 1926*

2 *Catch 22, by Joseph Heller*

3 *Mohandas*

4 *Sergei Eisenstein*

5 *Hitler, Chamberlain, Mussolini and Daladier*

6 *Berry Gordy*

7 *Moscow Art Theatre*

8 *67½ new pence*

9 *Alexander Kerensky*

10 *Katharine Hepburn – four*

11 *Vatican City, Switzerland and Monaco*

12 *Angela Mortimer, Anne Jones and Virginia Wade*

13 *Bretton Woods, 1944*

14 *His brother Ira Gershwin*

15 *George VI, in 1936*

16 *Valentina Tereshkova, in 1963*

17 *The Marne*

18 *Rob Reiner*

19 *Andrew Motion, Ted Hughes, Sir John Betjeman*

20 *Lord Rothschild*

1 Who wrote *The Prime of Miss Jean Brodie*?

2 In which two films did Bing Crosby sing *White Christmas*?

3 In which year did Britain legalise homosexuality?

4 Which four Irishmen were awarded Nobel Prizes for literature between 1923 and 1995?

5 On which day of the week did the Wall Street Crash begin?

6 Who shocked New York by exhibiting a urinal in an art gallery?

7 What was the full name for the Nazi Party?

8 What is Bob Dylan's real name?

9 What did Britain have 29 of in 1914 and Germany 17?

10 Who played Jolyon 'Jo' Forsyte in the BBC's Forsyte Saga series?

11 Who led the 1911 revolution in China?

12 Which two people cut the ribbons to open the Channel Tunnel in 1994?

13 Who was boss of Ealing Studios during its '40s and '50s heyday?

14 Who was Chief of the Imperial General Staff for most of the Second World War?

15 What was Timothy Leary's slogan for the '60s?

16 What was set up by seven countries in 1959 in opposition to the EEC?

17 Who made the first non-stop flight across the Atlantic?

18 Who wrote *One Flew over the Cuckoo's Nest*?

19 Who was the 'Empress of the Blues'?

20 Who wrote *An Actor Prepares* and *Building A Character*?

1   *Muriel Spark*

2   Holiday Inn *and* White Christmas

3   *1967*

4   *W.B.Yeats, George Bernard Shaw, Samuel Beckett and Seamus Heaney*

5   *'Black'Thursday, October 24, 1929*

6   *The dada artist Marcel Duchamp in 1917*

7   *National Socialist German Workers' Party*

8   *Robert Zimmerman*

9   Dreadnought *battleships*

10   *Kenneth More*

11   *Sun Yat-Sen*

12   *Queen Elizabeth and President Mitterand*

13   *Michael Balcon*

14   *Lord Alanbrooke*

15   *'Tune In, Turn On, Drop Out'*

16   *European Free Trade Association*

17   *Alcock and Brown, in 1919*

18   *Ken Kesey*

19   *Bessie Smith*

20   *Konstantin Stanislavski*

1 Where is the film *The Full Monty* set?

2 What was the wealthy class of Russian peasants liquidated in their millions in the '30s called?

3 Who said:'I was never an angry young man'?

4 Who wrote the music for the ballet *The Rite of Spring*?

5 How many goals did Bobby Charlton score in his 106 appearances for England?

6 Where did Martin Luther King make his 'I have a dream' speech?

7 In which year was the film *Saturday Night Fever* released?

8 Who was Britain's first woman Cabinet minister?

9 What are the world's six most populous countries?

10 Which forward-looking movement in the arts did the Italian poet Marinetti launch in a manifesto?

11 Which was Spain's only permitted political party under Franco?

12 What is Lady Chatterley's first name?

13 Which New Zealander was the first person to break the three-minutes-fifty-seconds barrier for the mile?

14 What was the name of the landing capsule used in the first manned landing on the moon?

15 What are the titles of the four *Star Wars* films?

16 What do the words 'menshevik' and 'bolshevik' mean?

17 Who wrote the lyric to the song *My Way*?

18 What does the system called Labanotation, invented in the '20s, record?

19 For which circus film did Cecil B. DeMille win a Best Picture Oscar?

20 Which offensive was launched in Vietnam on 30 January 1968?

1 Sheffield

2 Kulaks

3 Kingsley Amis

4 Stravinsky

5 49

6 By the Lincoln Memorial, Washington DC

7 1977

8 Margaret Bondfield, minister of labour under Ramsay MacDonald

9 China, India, USA, Indonesia, Brazil, Russia

10 Futurism

11 Traditionalist Spanish Falange

12 Constance or Connie

13 John Walker

14 The Eagle

15 Star Wars, The Empire Strikes Back, Return of the Jedi, The Phantom Menace

16 Minority and majority

17 Paul Anka

18 The steps of ballet dancers

19 The Greatest Show on Earth

20 The Tet Offensive

1   In which film did Marilyn Monroe's dress billow up over a subway vent?

2   Where were the Olympics held at which Ben Johnson was disqualified for taking drugs?

3   Who was Richard Nixon's chief of staff during the Watergate affair?

4   Which Chuck Berry classic begins: 'Deep down in Louisiana close to New Orleans'?

5   Which is the last surviving Stalinist state?

6   What are the novels in the trilogy by Mervyn Peake recounting the life of the 77th Earl of Groan?

7   In which battle did 420,000 Britons, 195,000 Frenchmen and 650,000 Germans lose their lives?

8   Who were the four British prime ministers who held office during the '50s?

9   What were Duke Ellington's first names?

10 What was the name of the building from which Lee Harvey Oswald shot President Kennedy?

11 In which city did Ann Frank and her family hide from the Nazis?

12 Which opera takes place in Catfish Row?

13 Which character did Marlon Brando play in the film *A Streetcar Named Desire*?

14 Which knighted British jockey rode a record 269 winners in 1947?

15 What is the name of the lion in *The Lion, the Witch and the Wardrobe*?

16 What was ENIAC?

17 Which Hitchcock film title paraphrases a quote by Hamlet?

18 What shortened many journeys by ship in August 1914?

19 Who designed the Seagram Building in New York?

20 Who fled to the Dominican Republic on 1 January 1959?

1   The Seven Year Itch

2   *Seoul, in 1988*

3   *Bob Haldeman*

4   Johnny B. Goode

5   *North Korea*

6   Titus Groan, Gormenghast *and* Titus Alone

7   *The Somme, 1916*

8   *Clement Atlee, Sir Winston Churchill, Sir Anthony Eden and Harold Macmillan*

9   *Edward Kennedy*

10   *The Texas School Book Depository*

11   *Amsterdam*

12   Porgy and Bess

13   *Stanley Kowalski*

14   *Sir Gordon Richards*

15   *Aslan*

16   *The world's first general purpose fully electronic digital computer*

17   North By Northwest *('I am but mad north-north-west')*

18   *The opening of the Panama Canal*

19   *Mies van der Rohe*

20   *Cuban dictator General Fulgencio Batista after Castro came to power*

1   Who was the first man to sail through the Northwest Passage?

2   Where is the film *Trainspotting* set?

3   What name was given to the strip of land that separated East Prussia from the rest of Germany after the First World War?

4   Who founded the US firm Wal-Mart, the world's most powerful retailer?

5   What are the nicknames of the Spice Girls?

6   Who was the first woman to head MI5?

7   Which runner did Zola Budd trip up at the Los Angeles Olympics of 1984?

8   Who was king of the Belgians from 1951 to 1993?

9   Who first developed an effective vaccine against polio?

10   Which Chinese leader resigned five months after sanctioning the Tiananmen Square massacre?

11   Which two people was O.J. Simpson accused of murdering?

12   In which city did Carlos the Jackal seize 11 oil ministers, including Sheikh Yamani of Saudi Arabia?

13   Who wrote *A Brief History of Time*?

14   Which American and which Frenchman are credited with discovering the HIV virus?

15   Who is in charge of the trains in *Thomas the Tank Engine*?

16   What feat of engineering, stretching 4,607 miles, was finally completed in 1904 after 13 years of building work?

17   Which magazine announced its closure in 1992 after 150 years of publication?

18   Jack Niklaus was the first golfer to win the US Masters in successive years. Who, in 1990, became the second?

19   How long is the Channel Tunnel?

20   What was the first cure for syphilis, patented by Dr Paul Ehrlich in 1907?

1   *Roald Amundsen, in 1903-6*

2   *Edinburgh*

3   *Polish Corridor*

4   *Sam Walton*

5   *Baby, Scary, Sporty, Posh*

6   *Stella Rimington*

7   *Mary Decker*

8   *King Baudouin*

9   *American microbiologist Jonas Salk, in 1954*

10   *Deng Xiaoping*

11   *Nicole Brown Simpson (his wife) and Ronald Goldman*

12   *Vienna, from OPEC's headquarters, in 1975*

13   *Stephen Hawking*

14   *Luc Montagnier of the Pasteur Institute, in 1983, and Robert Gallo in 1984, independently*

15   *The Fat Controller*

16   *The Trans-Siberian Railway*

17   *Punch*

18   *Nick Faldo*

19   *50 kilometres (31 miles)*

20   *Salvarsan*

1   What was the name of the East German secret police?

2   For which ballet dancer did the choreographer Mikhail Fokine create the Dying Swan solo?

3   The last volume – making around 120,000 new words in all – was finally completed in 1986. What was it?

4   What are the names of the Teenage Mutant Hero Turtles?

5   Which two politicians did John Major defeat to become prime minister in the Tory leadership ballot of 27 November 1990?

6   Who were the only three British men to win the Olympic 100 metres?

7   Who is the most widely syndicated cartoonist in history?

8   Who had a band called the *Revolution*?

9   Who wrote *The Color Purple*?

10 Rivalry between which two tribes has been responsible for the conflict in Rwanda?

11 Who invented the hovercraft?

12 Which sheikdom is controlled by the horse-racing Maktoum family?

13 Which scientist sent rockets to bomb London and man to the moon?

14 Who won costume design Oscars for the films *Gigi* and *My Fair Lady*?

15 What was the code name for the evacuation of Dunkirk by British and French forces in May and June 1940?

16 Which Californian county is known as Silicon Valley?

17 Which TV series was set in Eaton Place, Belgravia?

18 What was the 'shock' result of the 1950 soccer World Cup match played on 28 June?

19 Which fairytale opera is written for narrator and orchestra?

20 Which bombed city was the subject of a large oil painting by Picasso?

1 Stasi

2 Anna Pavlova

3 A Supplement to the Oxford English Dictionary

4 Michelangelo, Donatello, Leonardo and Raphael

5 Michael Heseltine and Douglas Hurd

6 Harold Abrahams, 1924, Alan Wells, 1980 and Linford Christie, 1992

7 Charles M. Schulz, creator of Peanuts. His work has appeared in over 2,300 newspapers

8 Prince

9 Alice Walker

10 Hutu and Tutsi

11 Christopher Cockerell

12 Dubai

13 Wernher von Braun, who developed the V2 rocket for Hitler and also the Saturn V rocket used in the Apollo programme

14 Sir Cecil Beaton

15 Operation Dynamo

16 Santa Clara

17 Upstairs Downstairs

18 England 0, USA 1

19 Peter and the Wolf, by Prokofiev

20 Guernica

1 Who was proclaimed Emperor of India in January 1903?

2 What name is given to the brief period of liberalism in Czechoslovakia prior to its invasion by Soviet troops in August 1968?

3 Which American dancer became the talk of Paris in 1925?

4 Who is the only Irish author to win the Booker Prize?

5 Who was Britain's defence secretary when Argentina invaded the Falklands?

6 Who conducted the Three Tenors at their 1990 World Cup open-air concert in Rome?

7 What is the title of Andrew Morton's first book about the Princess of Wales?

8 Who was Britain's first woman MP?

9 Which two colours does Dennis the Menace always wear?

10 What is the name of the character played by Glenn Close in *Fatal Attraction*?

11 What is the title of Primo Levi's book, published in 1947, about his experiences in the concentration camp of Auschwitz?

12 What name was given to the method of bulk production of ammonia from atmospheric nitrogen and hydrogen that helped Germany manufacture explosives in the First World War?

13 Which country was expelled from the United Nations in 1971?

14 Which SAS hero led the UN peacekeeping force in Bosnia?

15 What was the title of the poet Robert Graves's frank autobiography?

16 Who was the first modern 'royal' to become a Catholic?

17 Who were the two founders of Microsoft?

18 Who has won the most motorcycle world championship titles?

19 In which yacht did Francis Chichester sail around the world in 1967-8?

20 Outside which town is Anthony Gormley's *Angel of the North*, Britain's biggest sculpture?

1 *King Edward VII*

2 *The Prague Spring*

3 *Josephine Baker*

4 *Roddy Doyle, in 1993, for* Paddy Clarke Ha Ha Ha

5 *John Nott*

6 *Zubin Mehta*

7 Diana, Her True Story

8 *Lady Astor, in 1919*

9 *Red and black*

10 *Alex Forrest*

11 If This Is a Man

12 *Haber-Bosch process*

13 *Taiwan, when Communist China was admitted*

14 *Sir Michael Rose*

15 Goodbye to All That

16 *The Duchess of Kent, in 1994*

17 *Bill Gates and Paul Allen*

18 *Giacomo Agostini of Italy, 15*

19 Gipsy Moth IV

20 *Gateshead*

1 Who was China's prime minister from 1949–76 and its foreign minister from 1949–58?

2 What is the title of Nelson Mandela's autobiography?

3 In which country was the trader Nick Leeson operating when he brought down Barings Bank?

4 What is the first name of golfer 'Tiger' Woods?

5 For writing which book about the Russian labour camp system was Alexander Solzhenitsyn expelled from the Soviet Union?

6 Who produced the film *Gone With the Wind*?

7 Which country was ruled by the hardliner Todor Zhivkov?

8 In which Gloucester street did murderers Fred and Rosemary West live?

9 What was the name of the secret police force and militia run by 'Papa Doc' and 'Baby Doc' Duvalier in Haiti?

10 Which actor won his first Oscar at the age of 77?

11 Which of the Mitford sisters married Oswald Mosley?

12 What was the name of the Foreign Minister who resigned in the wake of the Argentine invasion of the Falklands?

13 Who writes the Mr Men books?

14 Which was the last of the elementary particles known as Quarks to be discovered following a 20-year search?

15 Who was the first US president to make an official visit to China?

16 What is the name of James Brown's backing band?

17 Which country ruled Palestine until 1918?

18 Which Italian painter, who specialised in nudes, died in 1920 of drink, drugs and TB?

19 Who was the highest-paid sportsman of the 20th century?

20 Which great Russian-American choreographer died in 1983?

1   Zhou Enlai (Chou En-lai)

2   Long Walk to Freedom

3   Singapore

4   Eldrick

5   Gulag Archipelago

6   David O. Selznick

7   Bulgaria

8   Cromwell Street

9   Tontons Macoutes

10 Henry Fonda, for On Golden Pond

11 Diana

12 Lord Carrington

13 Roger Hargreaves

14 Top, in 1994

15 Richard Nixon, in 1972

16 The Famous Flames

17 Turkey

18 Amedeo Modigliani

19 Michael Jordan, who earned over $300 million

20 George Balanchine

1   Which modern country is the site of the world's earliest known civilization, the Sumerian?

2   What is the condition myalgic encephalomyelitis usually called?

3   Who was Germany's foreign minister during the Second World War?

4   Which 400-year rift ended with an historic meeting in Italy on 23 March 1966?

5   Who won the Turner Prize for an inside-out house in 1993?

6   Who sang the line: 'They paved Paradise and put up a parking lot'?

7   What did it say on the notice that President Harry S. Truman always kept on his desk?

8   Who was the first Black American to win a Nobel prize for literature?

9   What was the name of Britain's first boutique, opened by Mary Quant in King's Road, Chelsea?

10 Who was the US Secretary of State for much of the '50s, responsible for developing much of the country's Cold War policy?

11 Which was the first James Bond film?

12 Who were Roger Bannister's pacemakers when he ran the first sub four-minute mile?

13 What does 'Yugoslavia' mean?

14 What do the initials stand for in Einstein's formula $E = mc^2$?

15 Which was the first televised trial, held in 1961?

16 In which year did the play The Mousetrap open in London?

17 Who spent 12 days talking peace at Camp David in September 1978?

18 What is the botanical term for marijuana?

19 Whom did prime minister Harold Wilson meet for talks on the HMS Tiger in December 1966?

20 Who were the three silent movie stars involved in founding the United Artists film company?

1 Iraq

2 'Yuppie flu' or ME

3 Ribbentrop

4 The rift between the Roman Catholic and Anglican churches, which ended when the Pope and the Archbishop of Canterbury had an official meeting and worshipped together in St. Peter's

5 Rachel Whiteread

6 Joni Mitchell

7 'The buck stops here!'

8 Toni Morrison

9 Bazaar

10 John Foster Dulles

11 Dr No, in 1962

12 Chris Brasher and Christopher Chataway

13 Land of the southern Slavs

14 E – energy, m – mass, c – speed of light

15 The trial of Adolf Eichmann in Israel for war crimes

16 1952

17 Prime minister Menachem Begin of Israel and president Anwar Sadat of Egypt

18 Cannabis sativa

19 Rhodesian prime minister Ian Smith after his Unilateral Declaration of Independence

20 Charles Chaplin, Mary Pickford, Douglas Fairbanks

1 Which novel about the hardships of the Joad family came out to acclaim in the '30s?

2 Where was the first successful coup in Western Europe after the end of the Second World War?

3 Who was the first player to hit six 'sixes' in one over in first-class cricket?

4 Who was commander in chief of Bomber Command from 1942 until the end of the war?

5 What is the French term for their ultra high-speed trains?

6 In which movie did Bob Hope play Turkey Jackson to Dorothy Lamour's Princess Shalmar?

7 What was the year of the 'Black Monday' stock market crash when the Dow Jones index crashed by over 20 per cent?

8 Which company made the Comet, the first jet airliner to make commercial flights?

9 Which Turkish leader abolished the fez?

10 Which Jewish terrorist group blew up Jerusalem's King David Hotel?

11 How did the poet Rupert Brooke die?

12 What were the first names of the three suffragette Pankhursts?

13 What is the name of the central character of *Roots*?

14 Who were the four original members of *The Who*?

15 Which golfer has won the most Majors?

16 Who was principal conductor of the Berlin Philharmonic for over 30 years?

17 In which Bond film does Oddjob appear?

18 Which countries were separated by the treaty of St Germain?

19 With which art form do you associate Naum Gabo?

20 Who produced the 'wall of sound' records *You've Lost That Lovin' Feeling* and *River Deep Mountain High*?

1   The Grapes of Wrath, *by John Steinbeck*

2   *Greece, in 1967 when the colonels came to power*

3   *Gary Sobers for Notts against Glamorgan in 1968*

4   *Arthur 'Bomber' Harris*

5   *TGV – Train à grande vitesse*

6   **Road to Morocco**

7   *1987*

8   *De Havilland*

9   *Mustafa Kemal Ataturk*

10   *Irgun Zvai Leumi, in July 1946*

11   *Of blood poisoning in Greece while on his way to fight in the First World War*

12   *Emmeline, and daughters Christabel and Sylvia*

13   *Kunta Kinte*

14   *Pete Townsend, John Entwistle, Roger Daltrey and Keith Moon*

15   *Jack Nicklaus, 18*

16   *Herbert von Karajan*

17   *Goldfinger*

18   *Austria and Hungary, in 1919*

19   *Abstract sculpture*

20   *Phil Spector*

1 Who was the first 20th-century US president to be sworn in because of an assassination?

2 Who sang *Uptight* (Everything's Alright)?

3 Who was the first athlete in Olympic history to receive a perfect score of ten?

4 How long did the first powered flight by the Wright brothers last?

5 Who appointed Hitler as chancellor of Germany in 1933?

6 Whose horse did suffragette Emily Davison throw herself under?

7 What is the family name of the emir of Kuwait?

8 What are the books in Tolkien's *Lord of the Rings* trilogy?

9 What is the full term for CFC gases?

10 With whom did Mark Norman write the screen play for *Shakespeare in Love*?

11 Which space shuttle exploded in 1986 killing its crew of seven?

12 Who led the Back to Africa movement in America that greatly influenced Rastafarianism?

13 What was escapologist Harry Houdini's real name?

14 Which film director, born in 1875, helped develop the closeup, the long shot, the flashback and the fadeout?

15 Who assassinated Mahatma Gandhi?

16 What was Madonna's first hit record?

17 Who banned music in Afghanistan and made beards compulsory for men?

18 Which dissident Russian scientist was exiled to Gorky in 1980?

19 Which jazz style did Charlie Parker and Dizzy Gillespie invent?

20 Which novel begins: 'Granted: I am an inmate of a mental hospital; my keeper is watching me'?

1   Theodore Roosevelt after the assassination of William McKinley in 1901

2   Stevie Wonder

3   Gymnast Nadia Comaneci at Montreal in 1976

4   12 seconds

5   Paul von Hindenburg, the president of the Weimar Republic

6   George V's, at the 1913 Derby

7   al-Sabah

8   The Fellowship of the Ring, The Two Towers and The Return of the King

9   Chlorofluorocarbons

10 Tom Stoppard

11 Challenger

12 Marcus Garvey

13 Eric Weiss

14 D.W. Griffith

15 Hindu extremist Nathuran Godse

16 Like a Virgin

17 The Taliban

18 Andrei Sakharov

19 Be Bop

20 The Tin Drum, by Günter Grass

1   What were the first three words ever spoken in a movie?

2   Which were the six main opposing powers that went to war in Europe in 1914?

3   What is France's top prize for literature?

4   What was the slogan of the miners' leader A. J. Cook during the General Strike?

5   Who is the chief character in the works of Mickey Spillane?

6   Which British-based American bombers were used in President Reagan's 1986 attack on Libya?

7   Over which distances did Seb Coe set three world records in July and August 1979?

8   What did the 18th amendment to the US constitution ban?

9   Which place of entertainment closed in 1644 and re-opened in 1996?

10   What is the Polish term for Solidarity?

11   Which director and which painter collaborated on the classic '20s surrealist movie *Un Chien Andalou*?

12   What is the record for the most runs ever scored in a first-class cricket innings, held by Brian Lara?

13   What is the name of the boy who befriends E.T. in *E.T. The Extra-Terrestrial*?

14   Which animal marks the year 2000 in the Chinese calender?

15   Which Nazi leader built up the Luftwaffe?

16   Which diva was the first professional singer to perform for a fee on radio?

17   Which dictator and his wife were executed on Christmas day 1989?

18   Which 1928 lesbian novel was the subject of an obscenity trial?

19   Where did Torvill and Dean perform their Olympic Bolero routine?

20   Which patriotic film classic did Noel Coward write, co-direct and act in?

1 `Wait a minute!...(You ain't heard nothin' yet!') by Al Jolson in The Jazz Singer (1927)

2 The Allied Powers of Britain, France and Russia against the Central Powers of Germany, Austria-Hungary and Turkey

3 Prix Goncourt

4 'Not a penny off the pay, not a minute on the day'

5 The detective Mike Hammer

6 F-111s

7 800 metres, 1500 metres and mile

8 The sale, manufacture and possession of alcohol

9 The Globe Theatre

10 Solidarnosc

11 Luis Buñuel and Salvador Dali

12 501 not out

13 Elliott

14 Dragon

15 Goering

16 Nellie Melba, in 1920. She was paid £1000 for the session

17 Romanian dictator Nicolae Ceausescu and his wife Elena

18 The Well of Loneliness, by Radclyffe Hall

19 Sarajevo, in 1984

20 In Which We Serve (1941)

1   Which words appear on Magritte's famous painting of a pipe?

2   Which Archbishop of Canterbury married Charles and Diana?

3   Who succeeded Hitler after his suicide?

4   Who fought the 'Rumble in the Jungle'?

5   In which year did Soviet tanks roll into Hungary to suppress a nationalist uprising?

6   Which missiles were used to shoot down Iraq's Scuds in the Gulf War?

7   Which title did Tony Benn give up in order to sit in the Commons?

8   Who were the first three directors of the Royal Shakespeare Company?

9   Who were Britain's two prime ministers during the First World War?

10 Which pop music movement was founded by *Nirvana*?

11 Who founded the American Institute of Public Opinion?

12 Ann Jones was the first female left-hander to win Wimbledon. Who was the second?

13 What does the word 'Perestroika' mean?

14 What did the St Lawrence Seaway link when it opened in June 1959?

15 Which island was awarded the George Cross for resisting severe aerial bombardment during the Second World War?

16 Whose exhibit of the innards of a cow and her calf netted the £20,000 Turner Prize?

17 Who was president of Malawi from 1966 to 1994?

18 Which Irish artist died on 28 April 1992?

19 Who led the first Labour government in Britain?

20 Which historic port was besieged for weeks by Yugoslav federal forces in 1991?

1   Ceci n'est pas une pipe (this is not a pipe)

2   Dr Robert Runcie

3   Admiral Karl Dönitz

4   Muhammad Ali defeated George Foreman to regain the world title in October 1974 in Zaire

5   1956

6   Patriots

7   Viscount Stansgate

8   Peter Hall, Trevor Nunn and Terry Hands

9   Asquith and Lloyd George

10 Grunge

11 George Gallup

12 Martina Navratilova

13 Restructuring

14 The Great Lakes and the Atlantic Ocean

15 Malta

16 Damien Hirst's

17 Hastings Kamuzu Banda

18 Francis Bacon

19 Ramsay MacDonald

20 Dubrovnik

1 Which country music show is the oldest radio programme in the United States?

2 Which is the longest single-volume novel in English published in the 20th century?

3 Which two old enemies shook hands on the White House lawn on 13 September 1993?

4 Which three rock superstars died between September 1970 and July 1971?

5 Who was the first woman to head a Muslim state?

6 What does CD-ROM stand for?

7 Who were the two leaders of the 1916 Easter Rising in Dublin?

8 Which were the three films in which James Dean starred?

9 What name was given to the foreign volunteer force that fought on the Republican side during the Spanish Civil War?

10 Who took a record 19 wickets for 90 runs in a Test Match?

11 What went on show at the Cathedral of San Giovanni in August 1978?

12 What was the first full-length cartoon movie?

13 In which year did the UK join the EEC?

14 Where was the Earth Summit held?

15 What name was given to the atomic bomb dropped on Hiroshima?

16 Who were the four members of Led Zeppelin?

17 Which political leader of the 20th century holds the record for his works being most translated?

18 Which is the largest opera house in the world?

19 Which prime minister curbed the power of the House of Lords in 1911?

20 In which country did Mount Hudson erupt in 1991, destroying 15 per cent of the ozone layer over the Atlantic

1   The Grand Ole Opry

2   *Vikram Seth's* A Suitable Boy

3   *Yasser Arafat and Yitzhak Rabin*

4   *Jimi Hendrix, Janis Joplin and Jim Morrison*

5   *Benazir Bhutto, who became prime minister of Pakistan in 1988*

6   *Compact-Disc, Read-Only Memory*

7   *James Connolly of Sinn Fein and P.H. Pearse of the Irish Republican Brotherhood*

8   *Rebel Without a Cause,* East of Eden *and* Giant

9   *International Brigade*

10 *Jim Laker for England in July 1956 at Old Trafford*

11 *The Turin Shroud*

12 *Disney's Snow White and the Seven Dwarfs, 1937*

13 *1973*

14 *Rio de Janeiro, in 1992*

15 *Little Boy*

16 *Robert Plant, Jimmy Page, John Paul Jones and John Bonham*

17 *Lenin*

18 *The Metropolitan Opera House in New York*

19 *Asquith*

20 *Chile*

1   What was the year of the Queen's 'annus horribilis'?

2   Which four methods were used to assassinate Rasputin?

3   Which prime minister was born in Huddersfield?

4   Who was Soviet foreign minister during the Cuban missile crisis?

5   Which four players did Bjorn Borg defeat to win his five Wimbledon singles titles?

6   Which chancellor of the exchequer was famous for his 'austerity' policy?

7   Which Richard Strauss opera features the Marshallin and Oktavian?

8   Which is the odd one out among Ernest Hemingway, Adolf Hitler, Emile Durkheim and Tony Hancock?

9   Which telescope was launched into space on 25 April 1990?

10   Who starred opposite Gene Kelly in *Singing in the Rain*?

11   What was the nickname of the supreme commander of the Allied forces in the Gulf War?

12   Who shocked Wimbledon in 1933 by wearing shorts?

13   Who directed the film *The Piano*?

14   Which poet was put in an American psychiatric hospital for 12 years for broadcasting Fascist propaganda on Italian radio in the Second World War?

15   Who was the last emperor of China?

16   Who averaged 99.94 runs in a long Test career?

17   Who wrote the novel *Captain Corelli's Mandolin*?

18   Which Russian invented the helicopter in America?

19   To which London group of artists did Walter Sickert and Spencer Gore belong?

20   Who was the first prime minister of Israel?

1   *1992*

2   *He was poisoned, shot, stabbed and then dumped while still alive in the River Neva*

3   *Harold Wilson*

4   *Andrei Gromyko*

5   *Nastase, Connors(twice), Tanner and McEnroe*

6   *Sir Stafford Cripps*

7   *Der Rosenkavalier*

8   *Sociologist Durkheim wrote a study on suicide. The others committed suicide*

9   *The Hubble Telescope*

10   *Debbie Reynolds*

11   *'Stormin' Norman Schwartzkopf*

12   *The English men's finalist Bunny Austin*

13   *Jane Campion*

14   *Ezra Pound*

15   *Henry Pu-Yi*

16   *Sir Donald Bradman*

17   *Louis de Bernières*

18   *Igor Sikorsky*

19   *Camden Town Group*

20   *David Ben-Gurion*

1   Which designer introduced the 'New Look' for women in the late '40s?

2   What was the code name for Germany's invasion of the Soviet Union?

3   Whose world record lasted from 1968 until 1991?

4   Which Russian arts movement was founded by Vladimir Tatlin in the early years of the Bolshevik Revolution?

5   What is the binary number for 22?

6   What was the name of the plane in which Charles Lindbergh made the first solo nonstop flight across the Atlantic?

7   Who was war minister and prime minister of Japan from 1941 to 1944?

8   Which disease did the World Health Organisation declare to be eradicated in December 1980?

9   Which song spent a record 16 weeks at Number 1 in 1991?

10   Which weekly pastime did the British Baptist Union condemn in the '30s as 'injurious to moral sense and healthy sport'?

11   In which year did Britain adopt its decimal currency?

12   From which opera does the World Cup anthem *Nessun Dorma* come?

13   What was Joe Louis' nickname?

14   Where did the UK explode its first atom bomb?

15   What is the name of Audrey Hepburn's character in *Breakfast at Tiffany's*?

16   Which worldwide organisation of volunteers was founded by President Kennedy?

17   From which ballet company did Nureyev defect to the West?

18   Which Finnish athlete pulled off the double 'double' at the Montreal Olympics of 1976?

19   Which European emperor said in 1910: 'You see in me the last monarch of the old school'?

20   What does the acronym RADAR stand for?

20th Century

1. *Christian Dior*

2. *Barbarossa*

3. *Bob Beamon's long jump of 29 feet 2.5 inches*

4. *Constructivism*

5. *10110*

6. *Spirit of St Louis, 1927*

7. *Hideki Tojo*

8. *Smallpox*

9. *Everything I do, I do it for you, by Bryan Adams*

10. *The football pools*

11. *1971*

12. *Puccini's Turandot*

13. *The Brown Bomber*

14. *Monte Bello Islands off Australia*

15. *Holly Golightly*

16. *The Peace Corps*

17. *The Kirov*

18. *Lasse Viren, who successfully defended Olympic gold medals at 5000 metres and 10,000 metres*

19. *Franz-Joseph, Emperor of Austria-Hungary from 1848 until 1916*

20. *Radio detection and ranging*

20th Century

1   In which state was the Charleston born?

2   Who introduced universal secondary education to Britain?

3   What is the title of the Rupert Brooke poem that begins: 'If I should die think only this of me'?

4   How did escapologist Harry Houdini die?

5   In which country did the Mau Mau rebel against British rule?

6   Who invented Meccano?

7   What is Pope John Paul II's original name?

8   What name was given to the alliance between Germany and Italy created in 1936?

9   What is the name of the computer that kills its human masters in *2001: A Space Odyssey*?

10 Which British politicians formed the Gang of Four?

11 Which characters did Al Pacino, James Caan and Robert Duvall play in *The Godfather*?

12 Who was the first Director-General of the BBC?

13 From where did Marconi transmit the first wireless message across the Atlantic?

14 On which political platforms did Sir Oswald Mosley stand in Parliament?

15 What is the English title of Jean Paul Sartre's *L'Etre et le néant*?

16 Which Bolshevik newspaper was founded in 1912?

17 Which legendary jazz club was founded in Harlem in 1923?

18 How many judges were there at the Nuremberg trials?

19 Who wrote *The Railway Children*?

20 Which political party's name means 'soldiers of destiny'?

1   South Carolina – in Charleston

2   R.A.B. Butler, in 1944

3   The Soldier

4   His appendix burst

5   Kenya

6   Frank Hornby

7   Karol Wojtyla

8   Rome-Berlin Axis

9   HAL

10 David Owen, Shirley Williams, William Rogers and Roy Jenkins

11 Michael Corleone, Sonny Corleone and Tom Hagen

12 Lord Reith

13 The Lizard, Cornwall

14 He entered as a Conservative, became an Independent and then joined Labour

15 Being and Nothingness

16 Pravda

17 Cotton Club

18 Four – one each from the UK, USA, USSR and France

19 Edith Nesbit

20 Fianna Fail

1   Who in the '20s created the 'little black dress'?

2   In which year did the Victorian Age come to an end?

3   Which big '50s event featured a Dome of Discovery and a tower called the Skylon?

4   What is Margaret Thatcher's star sign?

5   Who were the assassins of John Kennedy, Robert Kennedy and Martin Luther King?

6   What are the names of the rootless young writer and his hero who go 'On the Road' in the novel by Jack Kerouac?

7   What are the names of the three inner forces that determine an individual's psychic life, according to Freud?

8   Which Briton took the world middleweight championship from Sugar Ray Robinson in 1951?

9   What stood at 4200 million to the US dollar at the end of 1923?

10   Who produced Michael Jackson's *Thriller* album?

11   For which achievement was Albert Einstein awarded the Nobel prize for physics?

12   How many symphonies did Sibelius write?

13   What was the last of President Wilson's Fourteen Points, designed to prevent a Second World War?

14   Who was England's cricket captain during the Bodyline tour?

15   What does the name Stalin mean?

16   Who founded the London Philharmonic Orchestra?

17   Which school was founded in Weimar in 1919, moved to Dessau in 1925 and closed when the Nazis came to power?

18   Did a round trip by air between Britain and Australia take more or less than a month in 1926?

19   Who designed the Morris Minor and the Mini Minor?

20   What is the full name of the character played by Orson Welles in Citizen Kane?

1 Coco Chanel

2 1901

3 The Festival of Britain, 1951

4 Libra

5 Lee Harvey Oswald, Sirhan Sirhan and James Earl Ray

6 Sal Paradise and Dean Moriarty

7 The id, ego and super-ego

8 Randolph Turpin

9 The German mark

10 Quincy Jones

11 The photoelectric law (and general services to theoretical physics)

12 Seven

13 The setting up of a League of Nations

14 Douglas Jardine

15 Steel

16 Sir Thomas Beecham

17 The Bauhaus school of architecture and design

18 More – 58 days

19 Alec Issigonis

20 Charles Foster Kane

1 Which large fish does the old Cuban fisherman catch in *The Old Man and the Sea?*

2 In which year did British women gain equal voting rights to men?

3 Which boxer had 49 fight and 49 wins?

4 In which area of Londonderry did British troops open fire on civil rights marchers on Bloody Sunday?

5 Who built the first solid-body electric guitar?

6 What is the name of Frasier's dog in the TV series?

7 Where were the peace talks held that led to the end of the war in Bosnia?

8 Who recorded Tamla Motown's first million selling record *Shop Around?*

9 Who succeeded Mao Tse-tung?

10 Who played Pharaoh to Charlton Heston's Moses in Cecille B. DeMille's *The Ten Commandments?*

11 Which jockey rode 8,833 winners?

12 To the nearest five shillings, how much did the Biro pen cost when it was launched in 1946?

13 Who were jointly awarded the Nobel Peace Prize for negotiating the Vietnam War cease-fire agreement?

14 In which decade did France abolish the guillotine?

15 Which solo instrument is heard at the very beginning of George Gershwin's *Rhapsody in Blue?*

16 The deciphering of 'Linear B' script in 1952 unlocked the secret of which Bronze Age civilization?

17 Which double agents did Sir Anthony Blunt help escape to the Soviet Union?

18 How many atoms of oxygen are there in a molecule of ozone?

19 What went missing in Paris on 22 August 1911?

20 What term did architects Alison and Peter Smithson coin for the uncompromising concrete and steel architecture of the '50s and '60s?

1   A marlin

2   1928

3   Rocky Marciano

4   Bogside, in January 1972

5   The musician Les Paul – marketed by the Gibson company

6   Eddie

7   Dayton Ohio in November 1995, leading to the Dayton peace accord

8   The Miracles, with Smokey Robinson

9   Hua Kuo-feng

10 Yul Brynner

11 American jockey Willie Shoemaker, between 1949 and 1990

12 55 shillings

13 Henry Kissinger and Le Duc Tho. Le Duc Tho declined to accept it

14 1980s

15 Clarinet

16 Minoan

17 Guy Burgess and Donald MacLean

18 Three

19 The Mona Lisa, when it was stolen from the Louvre

20 Brutalism

1   What is the name of the motel that Janet Leigh checks into in the film *Psycho*?

2   Where was the 'Velvet Revolution'?

3   What was found swimming off the coast of Madagascar about 60 million years after its supposed extinction?

4   Where was Britain's top secret Code and Cypher School during the Second World War?

5   Which Benjamin Britten opera is about a mad Suffolk fisherman?

6   Which scientist is known as the father of the hydrogen bomb?

7   Who were the four members of the Monkees?

8   Which general formally accepted the Japanese surrender in 1945?

9   What is the name of the pie shop in the television comedy *Blackadder*?

10   Who denounced whose 'cult of personality' in March 1956?

11   What was D.H. Lawrence's prequel to the novel *Women in Love*?

12   At which events did Zatopek win three gold medals at the Helsinki Olympics in 1952?

13   Which leader developed the policy of Ostpolitik to forge closer ties with the Eastern bloc?

14   Which three singers were killed in a plane crash on the 'day the music died' in February 1959?

15   In which year did Labour first win an overall majority in Parliament?

16   What is the name of Tony Blair's parliamentary constituency?

17   Who was the first black heavyweight boxing champion of the world?

18   Why was Stalin presented with a sword in 1943 as a gift from the king of England?

19   On which island was Prince Philip born?

20   With which artist did Picasso found Cubism?

1 Bates Motel

2 Czechoslovakia

3 A coelacanth, in 1938

4 Bletchley Park, Buckinghamshire

5 Peter Grimes

6 Hungarian born US physicist Edward Teller

7 Davy Jones, Mike Nesmith, Peter Tork and Mickey Dolenz

8 General MacArthur, Supreme Allied Commander in the South West Pacific

9 Mrs Miggins' Pie Shop

10 Soviet leader Krushchev denounced former Soviet leader Stalin

11 The Rainbow

12 5,000 metres, 10,000 metres and the marathon

13 West German chancellor Willy Brandt

14 Ritchie Valens, Big Bopper and Buddy Holly

15 1945 when Labour, under Clement Atlee, won the general election

16 Sedgefield

17 Jack Johnson, from 1908 until 1915

18 As a tribute to Russian heroism at the Battle of Stalingrad

19 Corfu

20 Georges Braque

1   What is the last line of the film *Some Like it Hot*?

2   How long did the General Strike last?

3   What did the initials of the smash hit radio programme ITMA stand for?

4   Which candidate's election headquarters did the Watergate burglars try to bug?

5   What do the initials stand for in P.G. Wodehouse?

6   Which invasion was codenamed 'Torch' in the Second World War?

7   Who played Holly Martins, the writer of tacky westerns, in the film *The Third Man*?

8   Which upper-class Buckingham Palace tradition took its last bow in March 1958?

9   Where was the first hydrogen bomb exploded?

10   Which company holds the world record for the biggest annual sales?

11   Who sang the line: 'You don't need a weatherman to know which way the wind blows'?

12   Which report called for social insurance in Britain 'from the cradle to the grave'?

13   Who was Britain's best known sculptor in the first half of the 20th century, whose tomb for Oscar Wilde was condemned as barbaric?

14   Which Australian-born son of a London University professor became a major Hollywood star, famous for roles such as Captain Blood?

15   Who headed the Vichy government in occupied France?

16   How did the French existential writer Albert Camus die?

17   Who issued the Downing Street Declaration offering Sinn Fein a role in deciding Northern Ireland's future if the IRA declared a ceasefire?

18   In which European country was the majority language not officially recognised until 1920 – 89 years after independence?

19   Who wrote *The Double Helix*?

20   How many bytes are there in a kilobyte of memory in computing?

1   'Nobody's perfect'

2   Nine days

3   It's That Man Again

4   Hubert Humphrey's

5   Pelham Grenville

6   The Allied invasion of North Africa in 1942

7   Joseph Cotten

8   The annual 'coming out' ceremony when debutantes would be presented to the Queen and Prince Philip

9   Eniwetok Atoll, Pacific Ocean, 1952, by the USA

10 General Motors – $168.8 billion in 1995

11 Bob Dylan

12 The Beveridge Report, 1942

13 Jacob Epstein

14 Errol Flynn

15 Marshall Philippe Pétain

16 The car he was in hit a tree

17 Irish prime minister Albert Reynolds and British prime minister John Major

18 Belgium, divided into a French-speaking minority and the Flemish majority

19 James Watson

20 1024

1 In which year did Bill Haley's *Rock Around the Clock* top the UK and American charts?

2 How many years were there between the first powered flight and the landing of men on the moon?

3 Who were the five original Marx Brothers?

4 What official position did Ronald Reagan hold when he testified before the Congressional Committee on Un-American Activities in the '40s?

5 Who was Poet Laureate from 1930 until 1967?

6 Which English football teams won the 'double' (League and FA Cup) in the 20th century?

7 At which convenient Alpine pass did Hitler and Mussolini meet up three times between March 1940 and June 1941?

8 Of which group of elements was Neptunium the first to be discovered, in 1940?

9 Which couple were dubbed 'the egghead and the hourglass'?

10 Which Oasis hit starts: 'Today is gonna be the day…'?

11 What was the name of the first nuclear powered submarine?

12 What was Judy Garland's real name?

13 Which leader did Idi Amin depose in a coup to come to power in Uganda?

14 Which father and son won Oscars for the film *Treasure of the Sierra Madre*?

15 Which American disc jockey coined the term Rock 'n' Roll?

16 What are the names of the Teletubbies?

17 Which leaders signed the SALT 1 agreements to limit nuclear weapons?

18 Which composer is renowned for scoring Hitchcock films?

19 To which organisation did John Logie Baird first demonstrate TV pictures of moving objects?

20 Who wrote his seventh symphony in Leningrad while under siege?

1 1955

2 66 years

3 Groucho, Chico, Harpo, Zeppo and Gummo

4 President of the Screen Actors Guild

5 John Masefield

6 Tottenham, Arsenal, Liverpool and Manchester United

7 The Brenner Pass, between Italy and Austria

8 Transuranium elements

9 Playwright Arthur Miller and his wife Marilyn Monroe

10 Wonderwall

11 The Nautilus, launched by the USA in 1954

12 Frances Gumm

13 Milton Obote

14 Actor Walter Huston and his son, director John Huston

15 Alan Freed

16 Dipsy, Tinky Winky, Laa-Laa, Po

17 Richard Nixon and Leonid Brezhnev

18 Bernard Herrmann

19 The Royal Institution, London

20 Shostakovitch

1 What is the population of the world?

2 Which movie musical does the song *Oh, What a Beautiful Morning* get off to a bright start?

3 Who was captain of the *Titanic*?

4 What is the term for abuse or rudeness directed at another person on the internet?

5 Which American general was known as 'Old Blood and Guts'?

6 To which class of drugs do valium and librium belong?

7 Who was the first Secretary General of the United Nations?

8 What happened in a cricket match between Australia and West Indies in December 1960 that had never before happened in Test cricket?

9 Which great Austrian composer died in 1911?

10 How many Arab-Israeli wars have there been since the founding of the state of Israel in 1948?

11 What was the title of Norman Mailer's first novel?

12 Who painted the 'modern old master' portrait of the Queen that drew a quarter of a million visitors to the Royal Academy's summer exhibition of 1955?

13 How is Joseph Djugashvili better known?

14 Who was the first singer to sell a million copies of a record?

15 Which post-war British politician served most terms as prime minister?

16 Which songwriting partnership penned *You'll Never Walk Alone*?

17 What do AM and FM stand for on a radio?

18 Who was the first Briton in space?

19 Which were the four main factions involved in the Lebanese civil war?

20 What is the cinematic link between William Makepeace Thackeray, Stephen King and Arthur C. Clarke?

1 Approximately six billion

2 Oklahoma

3 Edward Smith

4 Flaming

5 General George S. Patton

6 Benzodiazepines

7 The Norwegian, Trygve Lie

8 The match was tied

9 Gustav Mahler

10 Four (in 1948, 1956, 1967 and 1973)

11 The Naked and the Dead

12 Pietro Annigoni

13 As Stalin

14 Enrico Caruso, with Vesti la giubba from Leoncavallo's I Pagliacci

15 Harold Wilson, four (1964-6, 1966-70, 1974, 1974-6)

16 Richard Rodgers and Oscar Hammerstein

17 Amplitude modulation and frequency modulation

18 Helen Sharman

19 Druse, Sunni Muslims, Shi'ite Muslims, and Maronite Christians

20 All wrote books made into films by Stanley Kubrick: Barry Lyndon, The Shining and 2001 A
Space Odyssey

1 Which famous songwriter's first hit was *Keep the Home Fires Burning*?

2 How many Labour prime ministers has Britain had?

3 Who taught 'method' acting to Marlon Brando and other stars at the Actors Studio in New York?

4 Which country did the 38th parallel divide?

5 Who is the drop-out narrator of *The Catcher in the Rye*?

6 Which three countries attacked Egypt during the Suez Crisis?

7 What is the name of the block of flats that is home to Del Boy and Rodney in the television series *Only Fools and Horses*?

8 Which report recommended that homosexual acts between consenting adults in private be legalised in Britain?

9 To the nearest £50, how much did a Mini cost when the car was launched in 1959?

10 Who beat whom in the 'Matthews' final at Wembley in 1953?

11 What momentous event took place at a University of Chicago squash court on 2 December 1942?

12 Which writer ran away from his wife aged 82 and died at a railway station?

13 Which country did Italy occupy in 1939?

14 What are the four most commonly spoken languages in the world?

15 Which was the first James Bond book?

16 Who was the first president of independent Zambia?

17 What do Englishmen detest, according to Noel Coward's song *Mad Dogs and Englishmen*?

18 Who were the six members of the Monty Python team?

19 To which leader did the Queen remark in October 1994: 'You and I have spent our lives believing this could never happen'?

20 Which novel won Salman Rushdie the 1981 Booker prize?

1   Ivor Novello

2   Five (Ramsay MacDonald, Clement Attlee, Harold Wilson, James Callaghan, Tony Blair)

3   Lee Strasberg

4   Korea, into North and South in 1945

5   Holden Caulfield

6   Britain, France and Israel

7   Nelson Mandela House

8   Wolfenden Report, 1957

9   About £500

10 Blackpool, with veteran Stanley Matthews, came from behind to beat Bolton 4-3

11 The world's first controlled nuclear chain reaction

12 Leo Tolstoy

13 Albania

14 Chinese (Mandarin), English, Hindustani (Hindi) and Spanish

15 Casino Royale

16 Kenneth Kaunda

17 A siesta

18 John Cleese, Terry Gilliam, Graham Chapman, Terry Jones, Eric Idle, Michael Palin

19 President Yeltsin of Russia on the first occasion a British sovereign visited Moscow

20 Midnight's Children

1   Which explorer's last words were:'I am just going outside and may be some time'?

2   Which music hall star brought the house down with *Roamin' in the Gloamin'* at the 1912 Royal Command performance?

3   Which forbidden zone did German troops march into on 7 March 1936?

4   What attracted thousands to Yasgur's Farm, New York State in 1969?

5   Who wrote *The Wind in the Willows*?

6   Where and what is Bahia Cochinos?

7   Which society osteopath lived off the immoral earnings of Christine Keeler and Mandy Rice-Davies?

8   Who was the first man to beat Mike Tyson in a professional bout?

9   Who discovered the nucleus of the atom?

10   Who was the chief architect of the Red Army?

11   Which six republics made up Yugoslavia in 1990?

12   Who played the part of Fagin in David Lean's film of *Oliver Twist*?

13   The first of a planned half million went on show in London in April 1944. Each covered 616 square feet. What were they?

14   Who were the four members of the Goons?

15   Which southern African nation won independence on 21 March 1990 after 23 years of armed struggle?

16   Which knighted cricketer holds the record for the most runs ever scored in Test and county matches?

17   What is polytetrafluoroethene usually called in a kitchen?

18   Which actor said:'I can't emote worth a damn'?

19   What was the name of the government proclaimed by the Bolsheviks when they seized power in Russia in November 1917?

20   What was found at Sutton Hoo in 1939?

1 *Captain Laurence Oates in 1912, on leaving his tent to die rather than delay the rest of the group during Captain Scott's second expedition to the South Pole*

2 *Harry Lauder*

3 *The demilitarised zone of the Rhineland*

4 *The Woodstock pop festival*

5 *Kenneth Grahame*

6 *Bay of Pigs, Cuba, scene of the abortive CIA-backed coup to topple Fidel Castro in 1961*

7 *Stephen Ward*

8 *James 'Buster' Douglas*

9 *Ernest Rutherford*

10 *Leon Trotsky*

11 *Bosnia-Hercegovina, Croatia, Macedonia, Montenegro, Serbia and Slovenia*

12 *Alec Guinness*

13 *Prefab houses*

14 *Peter Sellers, Harry Secombe, Michael Bentine, Spike Milligan*

15 *Namibia*

16 *Sir Jack Hobbs, 61,237 runs*

17 *Teflon*

18 *Clark Gable*

19 *The Council of People's Commissars*

20 *A fabulous hoard of Anglo Saxon treasure contained in a ship-burial*

1 Which book by a Japanese-born writer is about an English butler?

2 What is the name of Dorothy's aunt in *The Wizard of Oz*?

3 Which three Indian prime ministers came from three successive generations of the same family?

4 Which two gases are normally used to fill fluorescent tubes?

5 What term was used to refer to the British forces sent to fight in France in 1914?

6 In which film does Jeanne Moreau jump into the River Seine?

7 What is the original German title of *The Threepenny Opera*?

8 Who said: 'A pint? Why, that's very nearly an armful'?

9 Who invented nylon?

10 Which school of psychology did Wolfgang Kohler and Kurt Koffka found?

11 Which Indian political organisation demanded an independent Muslim state in 1940?

12 What was the Windmill theatre's proud boast after the wartime air raids?

13 In which year did Margaret Thatcher introduce the Poll Tax in England and Wales?

14 Which composer wrote his seventh symphony for the film *Scott of the Antarctic*?

15 What are the names of the four characters in the TV series *The Young Ones*?

16 What did American surgeons suggest replace cocaine, chloroform and ether in anaesthetics at their New York conference in 1912?

17 Who were the 11 members of the England team that won the World Cup in 1966?

18 In which city was the PLO founded?

19 Which composer wrote the score to Olivier's film of Henry V?

20 What term is used to refer to 16 September 1992, when Britain pulled out of the ERM after losing billions of pounds defending sterling against currency speculators?

1   The Remains of the Day, *by Kazuo Ishiguro.*

2   *Aunt Em*

3   *Jawaharlal Nehru, his daughter Indira Gandhi and her son Rajiv Gandhi*

4   *Argon and mercury vapour*

5   *British Expeditionary Force ('the Old Contemptibles')*

6   *Jules et Jim*

7   *Die Dreigroschenoper*

8   *Tony Hancock in* The Blood Donor

9   *Wallace Carothers*

10 *Gestalt*

11 *The Muslim League*

12 *'We never closed'*

13 *1990*

14 *Ralph Vaughan Williams — Sinfonia Antarctica*

15 *Rik, Vyvyan, Neil and Mike*

16 *Nitrous oxide or 'laughing gas'*

17 *Banks, Cohen, Wilson, Stiles, Charlton (J), Moore, Ball, Hurst, Charlton (R), Hunt, Peters*

18 *Beirut, in 1964*

19 *William Walton*

20 *Black Wednesday*

1   Which neuro-transmitter does Prozac boost?

2   What is the official language of society in the novel *Nineteen Eighty-four*?

3   Which studio produced the film *The Wizard of Oz*?

4   Which highjumper launched 'the flop' at the 1968 Mexico Olympics?

5   Who wrote *Sexual Behaviour in the Human Female*?

6   To the nearest five million, what was the population of Great Britain in 1900?

7   Apart from the United States, which are the only two countries to have won the America's Cup yacht-racing trophy ?

8   Who was supreme commander of the Allied forces that invaded Europe on D-Day?

9   Who directed *Four Weddings and a Funeral*?

10   Who was the first criminal to be caught by means of radio?

11   Which discovery by Karl Landsteiner in 1900 made blood transfusions safer?

12   Which countries formed a European customs union in 1948?

13   Which came first: Picasso's Blue Period or his Rose Period?

14   Who wrote *Schindler's Ark*, on which the film *Schindler's List* is based?

15   For which television series did Nat Hiken write many of the scripts?

16   Which United Nations organisation is known by the initials IUCN?

17   Which is the cruellest month, according to TS Eliot in the first line of *The Wasteland*?

18   What is footballer Pele's real name?

19   Which theatre was launched by the poet W.B. Yeats in 1904?

20   What is the significance of 9,192,631,770 cycles of caesium vibration?

1   Serotonin

2   Newspeak

3   MGM

4   Dick Fosbury

5   Alfred Kinsey, in 1953

6   41 million

7   Australia (in 1983) and New Zealand (in 1995)

8   General Dwight D. Eisenhower

9   Mike Newell

10   Dr Crippen, arrested on board a ship off Canada by Scotland Yard detectives in 1910

11   ABO blood groups

12   Belgium Netherlands and Luxembourg, who formed Benelux

13   Blue Period (1901-4). The Rose Period was 1905-8

14   Thomas Keneally

15   Sergeant Bilko

16   International Union for the Conservation of Nature

17   April

18   Edson Arantes do Nascimento

19   Abbey Theatre, Dublin

20   It represents the international definition of a second

1   In which month of which year did the world hold its breath until Kruschev backed down in the Cuban missile crisis?

2   Which was the first film Humphrey Bogart and Lauren Bacall made together?

3   At which hotel did John Lennon and Yoko Ono hold their seven-day bed-in?

4   Which member of the Liberal government was president of the board of trade in 1908, home secretary in 1910 and first lord of the Admiralty in 1911?

5   At which Sheffield theatre is the snooker World Professional Championship held each year?

6   Which Russian won the 1906 Nobel Prize for work on the digestive system?

7   In which year did Elvis Presley die?

8   What was first used successfully at the Battle of Cambrai in November 1917?

9   Which Austrian psychologist originated the concept of the inferiority complex?

10 Which composer provides the music to the film *Brief Encounter*?

11 Which books by Elizabeth David in 1950 and 1951 are said to have revolutionised British eating?

12 To the nearest three million, how many people died in the flu epidemic of 1918-19?

13 Which publisher founded *Time*, *Life*, *Fortune* and *Sports Illustrated* magazines?

14 Who painted the murals in the Tate Gallery restaurant?

15 Which African country did Italy invade on 3 October 1935?

16 In which year was British India divided into India and Pakistan?

17 Which university college was founded by Sidney and Beatrice Webb?

18 What is the English title of the Proust masterpiece *À la recherche du temps perdu*?

19 What is the name of the sordid music hall comedian played by Laurence Olivier in John Osborne's *The Entertainer*?

20 Who was the world's first female prime minister?

1   October 1962

2   To Have and Have Not

3   Amsterdam Hilton

4   Winston Churchill. He later rejoined the Conservatives

5   The Crucible

6   Ivan Pavlov, for his experiments involving dogs

7   1977

8   The tank

9   Alfred Adler

10 Sergei Rachmaninoff

11 Mediterranean Food *and* French Country Cooking

12 About 20 million

13 Henry Luce

14 Rex Whistler

15 Abyssinia (now Ethiopia)

16 1947

17 The London School of Economics in 1895

18 Remembrance of Things Past

19 Archie Rice

20 Mrs Bandaranaike of Sri Lanka (1960-5, 1970-7)

1   Which novel is about a typical day in the lives of a Jewish advertisement canvasser and two other people on 16 June 1904?

2   Who led the team of scientists that produced the first atom bomb?

3   Who is the Governor of the Bank of England?

4   Which crown was used for the official act of crowning Queen Elizabeth II in Westminster Abbey?

5   Who said: 'A house is a machine for living in'?

6   What name was given to the political union of Germany and Austria in the '30s?

7   Oscar Wilde said he could resist anything except…what?

8   What are AGR and PWR reactors?

9   In which film do the members of a violent gang address each other as Mr Orange, Mr Blonde, Mr White and Mr Pink?

10 Who played both cricket and soccer for England?

11 What were the codenames of the five beaches used in the Normandy landings?

12 Which novel is set in the year 632 AF (After Ford)?

13 From which year until which year was Margaret Thatcher leader of the Conservative Party?

14 Which three scientists won the Nobel prize for developing penicillin?

15 Who holds the record for winning the Grand Prix World Drivers' Championship the most times?

16 What are the names of the two tramps in *Waiting for Godot*?

17 Who was the first man to reach the North Pole?

18 Who designed the VW Beetle?

19 What was remarkable about the instrumentation used on the Beatles song *Norwegian Wood*?

20 Who were Britain's three prime ministers in the Thirties?

1 Ulysses, by James Joyce

2 Robert J. Oppenheimer

3 Eddie George

4 St Edward's Crown

5 The architect Le Corbusier

6 The Anschluss

7 Temptation

8 Advanced gas-cooled reactors and pressurised-water reactors

9 Reservoir Dogs

10 Denis Compton

11 Utah, Omaha, Gold, Juno and Sword

12 Brave New World, by Aldous Huxley

13 1975–90

14 Alexander Fleming, Howard Florey and Ernst B. Chain

15 Juan Manuel Fangio (five times)

16 Vladimir (Didi) and Estragon (Gogo)

17 Robert Peary, in 1909

18 Ferdinand Porsche

19 It featured the sitar, the first use of an Indian instrument in pop

20 Ramsay MacDonald, Stanley Baldwin and Neville Chamberlain

1   What is the name of the great Jedi Master played by Sir Alec Guinness in *Star Wars*?

2   Which president freed Nelson Mandela from prison?

3   Who awakes one morning to find himself transformed into a giant insect?

4   Who chaired the investigation into the assassination of John F. Kennedy?

5   Which country won the first soccer world cup?

6   What is the full title of the AMPAS academy that presents the annual Oscars?

7   What do the initials of the BCG vaccine stand for?

8   Which Hollywood studio made the classic Astaire and Rogers musicals *Flying Down to Rio*, *The Gay Divorcee* and *Top Hat*?

9   Who was the first British king of the 20th century?

10   Which organisation was renamed the Labour Party in 1906?

11   Whose 1930 performance as *Hamlet* at the Old Vic was hailed as 'brilliant'?

12   At which hospital did Alexander Fleming discover penicillin?

13   Which ballet impressario first put on *The Firebird*?

14   What is the name of the character played by Charlie Chaplin in *The Great Dictator*?

15   Which extremist group was founded by Iranian Revolutionary Guards sent to Lebanon?

16   Which composer invented the 12-tone scale to make atonal music sound more coherent?

17   With which British record label did Bob Marley record ten albums?

18   Which parallel separated North Vietnam from South Vietnam?

19   Whom did Bobby Fischer defeat to become the first native-born American to win the world chess championship?

20   The foundations of which industry were laid in 1907 by Leo Baekeland?

1   *Obi-Wan Kenobi*

2   *F.W. de Klerk of South Africa, in 1990*

3   *Gregor Samsa, the hero of* Metamorphosis *by Franz Kafka*

4   *Earl Warren*

5   *Uruguay, in 1930*

6   *Academy of Motion Picture Arts and Sciences*

7   *Bacille Calmette Guerin, after the scientists who developed it*

8   *RKO*

9   *Edward VII*

10   *Labour Representation Committee*

11   *John Gielgud's*

12   *St Mary's Hospital, London*

13   *Sergei Diaghilev*

14   *Adenoid Hynkel*

15   *Hezbollah*

16   *Arnold Schoenberg*

17   *Island Records*

18   *The 17th parallel*

19   *Boris Spassky, 1972*

20   *Plastics*

1 In which year did the Berlin Wall go up, and in which year did it start to come down?

2 Which film featured Frank Sinatra, Bing Crosby and Louis Armstrong?

3 When did Halley's comet pay its last 75-yearly visit?

4 Who were the two leaders of the Soviet Union between Brezhnev and Gorbachev?

5 How did the previously unknown Louis Washkansky make history in 1967?

6 What do the initials PROM stand for in computing?

7 Which chancellor of the exchequer introduced premium bonds in 1956?

8 Which 21-year-old took over the Christian Dior design salon on the death of its founder Christian Dior?

9 Who exhorted his followers to be prepared to die if necessary in defiance of the hated British salt tax?

10 In which play did Noel Coward and Gertrude Lawrence smash gramophone records over each other's heads?

11 Who was the first man to complete a century of centuries while playing in a Test match?

12 Where does Graham Sutherland's gigantic tapestry *Christ in Glory* hang?

13 In which unusual place was Lyndon B. Johnson sworn in as president?

14 What name is given to the branch of astronomy that started with the Big Bang theory?

15 Which city has the highest murder rate in proportion to its population?

16 Which 1927 collaboration between Jerome Kern and Oscar Hammerstein II laid the foundations of the American musical?

17 What did inventor Frank Whittle patent in 1930?

18 Who wrote *A Year in Provence*?

19 What was the name of the militant section of CND which broke away from it in 1962?

20 In which Graham Greene novel does the character Scobie appear?

*C*20th*entury*

1   *1961 and 1989*

2   High Society

3   *1986*

4   *Yuri Andropov and Konstantin Chernenko*

5   *He received the first heart transplant*

6   *Programmable Read-Only Memory*

7   *Harold Macmillan*

8   *Yves St. Laurent*

9   *Mahatma Gandhi*

10 Private Lives, *by Noel Coward*

11 *Geoff Boycott, in 1977 against Australia*

12 *In Coventry Cathedral*

13 *On board the presidential jet Air Force 1 at Dallas after the assassination of President Kennedy*

14 *Modern cosmology*

15 *Bogota, Columbia, around 8,600 a year*

16 Showboat

17 *The jet engine*

18 *Peter Mayle*

19 *Committee of One Hundred*

20 The Heart of the Matter

1   What was Prime Minister Harold Macmillan's nickname?

2   Who wrote *A Hitchhiker's Guide to the Galaxy*?

3   From which country were 'Busby's Babes' returning home to England when their plane crashed in 1958?

4   What naval action of May 1915 led to anti-German riots in England and to American demands for a declaration of war?

5   What is the nickname of the rock 'n' roller Jerry Lee Lewis?

6   Who founded the 200,000-strong Unification Church, sometimes accused of brainwashing its members?

7   Which composer, who died in 1990, said he wanted to create music which would 'immediately be recognised as American'?

8   What was the name of Margaret Thatcher's economic adviser whose criticisms of Nigel Lawson led to the latter's resignation as Chancellor?

9   Which 1971 book was subtitled 'A savage journey to the heart of the American dream'?

10   Which woman toppled Ferdinand Marcos from power in the Philippines?

11   Which 22-year-old Soviet player became the youngest ever world chess champion in 1985?

12   Which Labour newspaper was launched in 1930?

13   Which planet did astronomer Clyde Tombaugh discover in 1930?

14   What was Cary Grant's real name?

15   Where was the Greenpeace ship *Rainbow Warrior* sunk by French secret agents?

16   Who created Andy Capp?

17   Who was Pope for just 33 days?

18   What is a more popular term for an integrated circuit or IC?

19   Which novel about a young doctor is told in three parts: I, Mosque; II, Caves, III; Temple?

20   Who led the French students in the 'month of the barricades' that rocked France in May 1968?

1   *Supermac*

2   *Douglas Adams*

3   *Yugoslavia, after defeating Red Star Belgrade*

4   *The sinking of the passenger liner* Lusitania *off the Irish coast by a German U-boat with the loss of over 1,100 lives*

5   *The Killer*

6   *Reverend Sun Myung Moon*

7   *Aaron Copland*

8   *Professor Sir Alan Walters*

9   Fear and Loathing in Las Vegas, *by Hunter S. Thompson*

10   *Mrs Corazon Aquino*

11   Gary Kasparov

12   The Daily Herald

13   Pluto

14   Archibald Leach

15   Auckland harbour, 1985

16   Reginald Smythe

17   John Paul I, who died soon after becoming Pontiff in 1978

18   Silicon chip

19   Passage to India, by E.M. Forster

20   Daniel Cohn-Bendit

1 What was the date of D-Day?

2 How many times has Brazil won the soccer World Cup?

3 What did Labour leader Tony Blair scrap on 29 April 1995?

4 What does the abbreviation MS-DOS stand for?

5 To whom was Britain's last surviving hangman Syd Dernley apprenticed?

6 Who was Britain's prime minister when India achieved independence?

7 Which winner of 41 Gand Prix races crashed to his death in 1994?

8 What is the former profession of Hannibal 'the Cannibal' Lecter in the film *Silence of the Lambs*?

9 What nationality is Carlos the Jackal?

10 What are the novels in Paul Scott's 'Raj Quartet'?

11 Who were the 'Big Three' leaders responsible for drawing up the Treaty of Versailles that set out the terms for peace with Germany after the First World War?

12 Which conductor plays himself in Disney's film *Fantasia*?

13 Who was the first African writer to win the Nobel Prize for LIterature?

14 Who recorded *The Message*, the first rap record to be voted Single of the Year by American rock critics?

15 Who choreographed the 1933 movie *42nd Street*?

16 At which number in Baker Street did Sherlock Holmes and Dr Watson live?

17 What was the surname that Malcolm X abandoned?

18 What is Woody Allen's real name?

19 To the nearest 30 cents, how many US dollars would you have got for one pound sterling in 1900?

20 Name either of the two bands with which Frank Sinatra made his name in his early years.

1   6th June 1944

2   Four times

3   Clause Four of Labour's constitution, committing the party to common ownership of the means of production

4   Microsoft Disc Operating System

5   Albert Pierrepoint

6   Clement Atlee, in 1947

7   Ayrton Senna

8   Psychiatrist

9   Venezuelan

10   The Jewel in the Crown, The Day of the Scorpion, The Towers of Silence, A Division of the Spoils

11   British Prime Minister Lloyd George, US President Woodrow Wilson and French Prime Minister George Clemenceau

12   Leopold Stokowski

13   Wole Soyinka, in 1986

14   Grandmaster Flash and the Furious Five, in 1982

15   Busby Berkeley

16   221b

17   Little

18   Allen Stewart Konigsberg

19   $4.87

20   Harry James Band and the Tommy Dorsey Band

1   Which American spy planes detected Soviet missile sites in Cuba?

2   Who was the first scientist to win two Nobel prizes?

3   Which comics publisher is associated with the heroes Superman, Batman and Wonderwoman?

4   What was Britain's last African colony?

5   Who wrote the novel *Jurassic Park*?

6   Which Australian and which American won the singles titles at the first Open Wimbledon in 1968?

7   Who was restored to the throne of a SE Asian country in 1993 – 38 years after abdicating?

8   In which country was Che Guevara born?

9   Which influential book, published in 1949, contained the line: 'One is not born a woman, one becomes one'?

10 What was the nickname of the governess to Princess Elizabeth and Princess Margaret who revealed royal secrets to an American magazine?

11 What was the former name of Malawi?

12 Who designed the Guggenheim Museum in New York?

13 Who became the first British golfer to win the US Open for 50 years, in 1970?

14 Which large piece of land did France acquire from Germany in 1919?

15 What did French and Italian tunnellers complete in 1962?

16 Which major invasion began with the 'Mukden incident' of September 1931?

17 What is the name of the young underworld character played by Richard Attenborough in the film *Brighton Rock*?

18 What was the name of the elite troops commanded by Rommel and defeated by General Montgomery at El Alamein, Egypt in 1942?

19 What have only Eddy Merckx, Bernard Hinault, Jacques Anquetil, and Miguel Indurain achieved?

20 Who wrote the books *Married Love* and *Wise Parenthood*, which caused a sensation when they came out in 1918?

1   U-2 planes, in 1961

2   Marie Curie, for physics in 1903 and for chemistry in 1911

3   DC Comics

4   Rhodesia, which achieved independence as Zimbabwe in 1980

5   Michael Crichton

6   Rod Laver and Billie Jean King

7   Prince Sihanouk of Cambodia

8   Argentina

9   The Second Sex, by Simone de Beauvoir

10 'Crawfie' (Marion Crawford)

11 Nyasaland

12 Frank Lloyd Wright

13 Tony Jacklin

14 Alsace and Lorraine

15 The Mont Blanc Tunnel under the Alps

16 The Japanese invasion of China

17 Pinkie Brown

18 Afrika Korps

19 Five victories in the Tour de France

20 Birth control pioneer Marie Stopes

1 Who wrote the words and who wrote the music in the Gilbert and Sullivan partnership?

2 What did the Holy Roman Emperor Francis II abolish in 1806?

3 Who discovered the secret of turning inanimate matter into animate matter at the university of Ingolstadt?

4 In which year was the Battle of Waterloo fought?

5 Which actor shot to fame playing Shylock at the Drury Lane theatre in January 1814?

6 Which two new radioactive elements did Marie and Piere Curie discover in pitchblende ores?

7 What is the name of Phileas Fogg's French valet in the novel *Around the World in Eighty Days*?

8 Which was the Year of Revolutions when revolts swept across Europe?

9 Which was the eldest Brontë sister?

10 What changed the face of cricket in 1864?

11 Who were the three founding members of the Pre-Raphaelite Brotherhood?

12 Which coded text lay unread for over a century in Magdalene College library before finally being deciphered and published in 1825?

13 Which group of landowners dominated Prussia's military elite?

14 What were Goethe's last words?

15 What did Sir Henry Bessemer's converter convert?

16 Who was given the *San Francisco Examiner* for his 18th birthday present?

17 In which sport was Fred Archer a great champion before shooting himself in 1886?

18 In which Norwegian verse drama does the Button Moulder try to melt the title character in his ladle?

19 Which four-times prime minister was disliked by Queen Victoria?

20 Which feat did Edward Whymper fail at seven times from the Italian side but finally manage from the Swiss?

1   W.S.Gilbert wrote the words and Arthur Sullivan wrote the music

2   The Holy Roman Empire

3   Frankenstein

4   1815

5   Edmund Kean

6   Polonium and radium

7   Passepartout

8   1848

9   Charlotte

10   The introduction of overarm bowling

11   Dante Gabriel Rossetti, Holman Hunt and John Everett Millais

12   The Diary of Samuel Pepys

13   The Junkers

14   'More light'

15   Iron into steel

16   William Randolph Hearst

17   Horse racing

18   Peer Gynt, by Henrik Ibsen

19   Gladstone

20   He climbed the Matterhorn

1 Which animals are Baloo, Bagheera and Shere Khan in Kipling's *The Jungle Book*?

2 What was the front page headline in the French *L'Aurore* newspaper on 13 January 1898, above Emile Zola's open letter to the head of the republic concerning the Dreyfus Case?

3 In which town was Picasso born?

4 Which non European city did British troops occupy and set on fire in August 1814?

5 Which opera is subtitled 'The Lass that Loved a Sailor'?

6 Which new dogma was decreed by the Vatican Council on 18 July 1870?

7 What did Gregor Mendel discover working with peas in a monastery garden?

8 Which British prime minister was known as 'Pam'?

9 Who was longest-serving Poet Laureate in the 19th century?

10 Which railway and shipping magnate opened the Grand Central Terminus in New York City?

11 Who entered Parliament in 1890 and stayed there for 55 years?

12 Which British scientist – who has a unit of measurement named after him – first demonstrated that heat and mechanical energy are different forms of the same thing?

13 Which French Post-Impressionist painted *The Bathers* and *Still Life with a Basket*?

14 Which Mexican dictator captured the Alamo after a fierce eleven-day battle?

15 Who founded Singapore?

16 Who is generally regarded as the first Conservative – as opposed to Tory – prime minister?

17 Which historical event is Tolstoy's novel *War and Peace* based around?

18 Which state did the USA buy from Spain in 1819?

19 Who discovered radioactivity in 1896?

20 Which novel was Dickens writing when he died?

1   *Bear, panther and tiger*

2   *J'Accuse*

3   *Malaga, in 1881*

4   *Washington, during the Anglo-American war*

5   *HMS Pinafore, by Gilbert and Sullivan*

6   *Papal Infallibility*

7   *The laws of genetics*

8   *Viscount Palmerston*

9   *Alfred Lord Tennyson (1850–92)*

10   *Cornelius Vanderbilt*

11   *Lloyd George*

12   *James Prescott Joule*

13   *Paul Cézanne*

14   *General Santa Anna*

15   *Sir Thomas Stamford Raffles in 1819*

16   *Sir Robert Peel*

17   *Napoleon's invasion of Russia in 1812*

18   *Florida*

19   *French scientist Henri Becquerel*

20   **The Mystery of Edwin Drood**

1   What did Nelson say immediately before the line 'Kiss me Hardy'?

2   In which southern state were the first shots of the American Civil War fired?

3   Which tiny particles were first isolated by the English physicist Joseph Thomson?

4   Which organisation was founded in London in 1864 to promote the interests of the working class?

5   Which novel features a flight through the Paris sewers by Jean Valjean?

6   Which Quaker, known for her work on prison reform, died in 1845?

7   Who published a revolutionary scheme for shorthand writing in 1837?

8   Whose rallying cry was 'Roma o Morte'?

9   The discovery of which diamond field in 1870 changed the course of South African history?

10   By which name was Emily Charlotte Le Breton, actress and mistress of the Prince of Wales, better known?

11   Which English chemist propounded the 'modern' atomic theory in 1808?

12   In which museum can you see Van Gogh's picture *The Potato Eaters*?

13   In which decade was the vacuum flask invented by the Scottish scientist Sir James Dewar?

14   With which Polynesian people did the British government negotiate the Treaty of Waitangi in 1840?

15   Which lazy character did the Russian writer Goncharov create?

16   Which opera was written for the opening of the Suez Canal?

17   Which German physicist gave his name to the dark lines in the solar system which reveal the chemical composition of the sun's atmosphere?

18   Who American poet wrote almost 2000 poems of which only two were published in her lifetime?

19   Which island was known as Van Diemen's Land?

20   Which organisation, founded in 1866 and still existing, was originally headed by former Confederate general Nathan Bedford Forrest?

1 'Take care of poor Lady Hamilton'

2 South Carolina

3 Electrons, in 1897

4 The First International, by Karl Marx

5 Les Misérables, by Victor Hugo

6 Elizabeth Fry

7 Isaac Pitman

8 Garibaldi's

9 Kimberley

10 Lily Langtry

11 John Dalton

12 Van Gogh Museum, Amsterdam

13 1870s

14 The Maori

15 Oblomov

16 Aida

17 Joseph von Fraunhofer, who mapped Fraunhofer lines

18 Emily Dickinson

19 Tasmania

20 The Ku Klux Klan

Where was Jack Worthing found as a baby in Oscar Wilde's *The Importance of Being Earnest*?

Which company did John D. Rockefeller incorporate in 1870?

From which Dorset village were six labourers transported to Australia in 1834 for forming a union?

Who is the laziest boy in Pinocchio's school?

Which two strategic waterways were the focus of the 'Straits Question' throughout the 19th century?

In what kind of factory was Dickens sent to work at the age of 12?

In 1804 Richard Trevithick built the first steam engine to do what?

Who composed the *Symphonie Fantastique*?

Which artist published *36 Views of Mount Fuji* and was a major exponent of *ukiyo-e*?

0 In which novel does John Ridd fall into the hands of an outlaw clan?

1 Which sport, first played in England in 1869, originated in Iran?

2 Which city did Tokyo replace in 1868 as capital of Japan?

3 Which drug-inspired work did Thomas de Quincey publish in 1821?

4 Who is usually referred to as the first Democrat president of the United States?

5 By which title did Max Aitken, born in 1879, become better known in later life?

6 Who was the first British king of the 19th century?

7 Which Danish scientist discovered electromagnetism in 1820?

8 What was the nickname of the resolute American Civil War general Thomas Jackson?

9 In which American state was the world's first oil well drilled at Titusville in 1859?

0 Which poet wrote: 'A thing of beauty is a joy forever'?

1   *In a handbag at Victoria Station*

2   *Standard Oil*

3   *Tolpuddle*

4   *Lampwick*

5   *Dardanelles and Bosphorus*

6   *A blacking factory*

7   *Run on rails*

8   *Hector Berlioz*

9   *Hokusai*

10   *Lorna Doone, by R.D. Blackmore*

11   *Polo*

12   *Kyoto*

13   *Confessions of an English Opium Eater*

14   *Andrew Jackson*

15   *Lord Beaverbrook*

16   *George III*

17   *Hans Oersted*

18   *'Stonewall'*

19   *Pennsylvania*

20   *John Keats*

1   Which character is always weeping in *Alice's Adventures in Wonderland*?

2   Which tsar emancipated the Russian serfs?

3   Which drug was first derived from the bark of the white willow tree?

4   Which aspect of the Earth did astronomer George Airy calculate by measuring gravity at the top and bottom of a coalmine?

5   In which novel does ignorant schoolmaster Wackford Squeers run Dotheboys Hall?

6   Who originated the Penny Post?

7   Which great violin virtuoso died in 1840?

8   Who produced the world's first petrol-driven motor vehicle?

9   Which five boroughs were formally linked in 1898 to create present day New York City?

10 In which county was the writer Thomas Hardy born?

11 Which congress of 1814-15 divided up Napoleon's empire after the Napoleonic wars?

12 Which university – famous for scientific research and education – was founded in Boston in 1861?

13 Whom did Alfred Lord Tennyson write about in his 10-book series of poems *Idylls of the King*?

14 Who was teacher Anne Sullivan's famous pupil?

15 Which south American country did Bernardo O'Higgins lead to independence?

16 Who was the first actor to be knighted?

17 Which means of scientific classification did Dmitri Mendeleyev devise in 1869?

18 Which British prime minister suppressed the Indian Mutiny?

19 Which monarch was Prince Regent before he became king?

20 How old did English geologist Arthur Holmes correctly calculate the Earth to be?

1   The Mock Turtle

2   Alexander II, in 1861

3   Aspirin

4   Its mass

5   Nicholas Nickleby

6   Rowland Hill

7   Niccolo Paganini

8   Karl Friedrich Benz

9   Manhattan, Brooklyn, The Bronx, Staten Island, Queens

10 Dorset

11 The Congress of Vienna

12 Massachusetts Institute of Technology

13 King Arthur

14 Helen Keller

15 Chile

16 Sir Henry Irving

17 The Periodic Table of elements

18 Viscount Palmerston

19 George IV

20 4.6 billion years

1 Who scored cricket's first triple century, in 1876?

2 Who used a dead cat to cure warts?

3 What are Victoria Crosses struck from?

4 Who designed the incomplete Church of the Holy Family in Barcelona?

5 Of whose death in 1805 was it said: 'men... turned pale as if they had heard of the loss of a dear friend'?

6 What is the name of Captain Ahab's ship in the novel *Moby Dick*?

7 Which leader's rallying call was 'blood and iron'?

8 In which novel would you find the character Little Nell?

9 What was first run in 1839, in Liverpool?

10 In 1882 and 1883 the scientist Robert Koch identified the bacteria that caused which two dangerous diseases?

11 Who wrote the Victorian best-seller *Missionary Travels*?

12 Where was General Gordon killed?

13 Which economic historian and social reformer coined the term 'Industrial Revolution'?

14 What is the name of Sherlock Holmes's brother whom he considers to be his master in the art of deduction?

15 Which Indonesian island was divided in 1859 between Portugal and Holland?

16 Which Tsar was immortalised in an opera by Mussorgsky?

17 Which layer of the Earth's atmosphere did Scottish physicist Balfour Stewart postulate the existence of in 1882 to account for differences in the Earth's magnetic field?

18 Who said: 'When I was a boy, the Sioux owned the world.'?

19 What did French naturalist Jean Baptiste de Lamarck hypothesise as the basic mechanism of evolution?

20 Which illness afflicted Dostoevsky?

1   *W.G. Grace*

2   *Tom Sawyer and Huck Finn*

3   *Bronze from guns captured from the Russians during the Crimean War*

4   *Antonio Gaudi*

5   *Nelson's*

6   Pequod

7   *Otto von Bismarck, Prussian prime minister and German chancellor*

8   The Old Curiosity Shop, *by Charles Dickens*

9   *The Grand National*

10 *Tuberculosis and cholera*

11 *Dr David Livingstone*

12 *Khartoum*

13 *Arnold Toynbee*

14 *Mycroft*

15 *Timor*

16 *Boris Godunov*

17 *Ionosphere*

18 *Chief Sitting Bull*

19 *The inheritance of acquired characteristics*

20 *Epilepsy*

1   Who spurns Heathcliffe in *Wuthering Heights*?

2   Which four nationalities defeated Napoleon at the Battle of Waterloo?

3   Was Queen Victoria over 43 or under 43 when Prince Albert died?

4   How did the Luddite wreckers of new machinery get their name?

5   Which technique of painting characterised by the use of small dabs was developed by post-impressionists Georges Seurat and Paul Signac?

6   Who is the son of the Mikado who falls in love with Yum-Yum in the opera by Gilbert and Sullivan?

7   What was the name of Van Gogh's brother, to whom he wrote a series of published letters?

8   How high is the 1050ft Eiffel Tower in metres?

9   How is the American fictional frontiersman Natty Bumppo better known?

10   Which English chemist discovered potassium, sodium, calcium, barium, magnesium and strontium?

11   What did the librarian Melvil Dewey do for literature?

12   Who painted the picture *Napoleon Crowning Josephine*?

13   What did Denmark give Sweden under the Treaty of Kiel in 1814?

14   What name is given to Balzac's series of over 40 novels, including *Père Goriot* and *La Cousine Bette*?

15   How many children did Queen Victoria have?

16   Who developed the first vaccine against rabies?

17   Who assassinated President Lincoln at Ford's theatre?

18   Who wrote the poem *Ode to the West Wind*?

19   Who was President of the Confederate States during the American Civil War?

20   Which company first demonstrated the feasibility of using pneumatic tyres on motor cars?

1   *Catherine*

2   *British, Prussians, Dutch and Belgians*

3   *Under – she was 42*

4   *Their public letters of protest were signed 'King Lud' or 'Ned Lud'*

5   *Pointillism*

6   *Nanki-Poo*

7   *Theo*

8   *322 metres*

9   *As Hawkeye*

10   *Sir Humphrey Davy*

11   *He originated the Dewey Decimal Classification system, widely used in libraries*

12   *Jacques Louis David*

13   *Norway*

14   *La Comédie Humaine*

15   *Nine*

16   *Louis Pasteur*

17   *John Wilkes Booth*

18   *Shelley*

19   *Jefferson Davis*

20   *Michelin*

1   What do the initials O.F.O.W. Wilde stand for in Oscar Wilde's full name?

2   Which major sport did James A. Naismith invent in 1891?

3   Which countries formed the Quadruple Alliance in 1813 against Napoleon?

4   Which of his characters did Dickens model on his father?

5   Which British inventor formed a company with Edison to make electric lamps in the UK?

6   Who proclaimed Queen Victoria empress of India?

7   Which pioneer route ran 2,000 miles from Independence Missouri to the Columbia River?

8   Of which newly-independent European country did the Great Powers elect Otto I of Bavaria to be king in 1832?

9   Which great composer carried Beethoven's coffin a year before his own death?

10   Who wrote: 'A population sodden with drink, steeped in vice…the denizens of darkest England among whom my life has been spent.'?

11   Who built 100 bridges in the north of Scotland alone?

12   Who wrote *The Swiss Family Robinson*?

13   What do the years 1832, 1867 and 1884 have in common in British history?

14   Which US president was the son of a US president?

15   What was the shape of the court when modern lawn tennis was first launched?

16   What is the name of the Tilney residence that forms the title of a novel by Jane Austen?

17   In which Chinese uprising did an estimated 60 million people die?

18   Who said on 18 June 1815: 'Everything failed me just at the moment when everything had succeeded.'

19   What were the names of the original Siamese twins?

20   Which city was besieged for a year during the Crimean War?

1 Oscar Fingal O'Flahertie Wills Wilde

2 Basketball

3 Austria, Britain, Prussia and Russia

4 Mr Micawber in David Copperfield

5 Sir Joseph Swan

6 Prime minister Benjamin Disraeli in 1876

7 The Oregon Trail

8 Greece

9 Franz Schubert

10 William Booth, founder of the Salvation Army

11 Thomas Telford

12 J.D. Wyss

13 They were all years of Reform Acts in which the franchise was extended

14 John Quincy Adams, son of John Adams

15 Like an hour-glass

16 Northanger Abbey

17 The Taiping Rebellion

18 Napoleon, at the Battle of Waterloo

19 Chang and Eng

20 The Russian city of Sevastopol on the Black Sea (1854-5)

1   Who took the first photograph?

2   What are the three Shakespeare operas by Verdi?

3   What begins: 'A spectre is haunting Europe – the spectre of communism'?

4   Who is beaten to death by the cruel overseer Simon Legree?

5   What is the next line of the popular Victorian music hall song that begins: 'We don't want to fight, but by Jingo if we do…'?

6   Which British king donated the royal menagerie to the Zoological Society in 1831?

7   What was the composer Rossini's first name?

8   Which statesmen represented Austria, France and Britain at the Congress of Vienna?

9   Who played the title role when Oscar Wilde's *Salomé* was premiered in Paris in 1893?

10   Which chief formed the Zulu Empire in Southeast Africa in 1818?

11   Which famous musical work commemorates the Italian novelist and patriot Alessandro Manzoni?

12   What is inscribed on a Victoria Cross?

13   Through which war did Britain acquire Hong Kong?

14   To which society, founded in 1884, did George Bernard Shaw and Sidney and Beatrice Webb belong?

15   Where did *phytophthora infestans* lead to over a million deaths?

16   What was Emily Brontë's pen name?

17   What are the three scripts on the Rosetta stone, which unlocked the secrets of ancient Egypt?

18   On which road did the flyin'-fishes play in the poem by Rudyard Kipling?

19   Which feat was the daring cross Channel swimmer Captain Webb attempting when he met his death?

20   Which poets eloped to marry in Italy?

1   *Joseph Niepce, in 1826*

2   Otello, Falstaff *and* Macbeth

3   The Communist Manifesto

4   *Uncle Tom, in* Uncle Tom's Cabin

5   *'We've got the ships, we've got the men, and got the money too.'*

6   *William IV*

7   *Gioacchino*

8   *Metternich, Talleyrand and Castlereagh/Wellington*

9   *Sarah Bernhardt*

10 *Shaka the Great*

11 *Verdi's* Requiem

12 *For Valour*

13 *First Opium War (1839–42)*

14 *Fabian Society*

15 *In Ireland, where it caused the potato blight that led to the famine of the 1840s*

16 *Ellis Bell*

17 *Greek, hieroglyphic and demotic*

18 *The road to Mandalay*

19 *Trying to swim the rapids below the Niagara Falls*

20 *Robert Browning and Elizabeth Barrett*

1   Who made the Gettysburg Address?

2   What is Rochester's first name in *Jane Eyre*?

3   What name is given to the 19th-century movement in Britain for universal male suffrage, annual parliaments, secret ballots and abolition of the property qualification for MPs?

4   Who wrote the libretto for Wagner's opera *The Ring*?

5   Who invented the electric telegraph?

6   Who had a vision in February 1858?

7   In which series of novels by Anthony Trollope would you find Archdeacon Grantly and Reverend Septimus Harding?

8   Which king made Arthur Wellesley the Duke of Wellington?

9   Which romantic composer wrote four symphonies and died in 1897?

10   The architect Louis Sullivan was dubbed 'the father' of what?

11   To which town were Huckleberry Finn and Jim travelling on their raft on the Mississippi?

12   Which industry did the aphid-like insect phylloxera nearly destroy in France?

13   Which impressario produced the first Gilbert and Sullivan operas?

14   Which English philosopher extended Darwin's theory of evolution and coined the phrase 'survival of the fittest'?

15   Which model village was founded in England in 1894?

16   Which Russian writer was killed in a duel?

17   What name is given to Beethoven's Ninth symphony?

18   Who wrote *Psychopathia sexualis*?

19   Which high street institution was originated by 28 poor men in Rochdale, known as the Rochdale Pioneers?

20   Who used the pseudonym Currer Bell?

1   President Abraham Lincoln after the Battle of Gettysburg, 1863

2   Edward

3   Chartism

4   Wagner

5   Samuel Morse, the inventor of morse code

6   St Bernadette of Lourdes

7   Chronicles of Barsetshire

8   George III

9   Johannes Brahms

10   The skyscraper

11   Cairo

12   The wine industry after it ravaged around two million hectares of vineyards

13   Richard d'Oyly Carte

14   Herbert Spencer

15   Bournville, by George Cadbury

16   Alexander Pushkin, in 1837

17   The Choral

18   Richard von Krafft-Ebing

19   The Co-op

20   Charlotte Brontë

1 Whose film of an oncoming train made an audience flee in panic in 1895?

2 Which prime minister said: 'I have climbed to the top of the greasy pole'?

3 Which Post-Impressionist painted the picture *Van Gogh Painting Sunflowers*?

4 Which novelist coined the term Wars of the Roses?

5 What name did the famous Russian goldsmith and jeweller Karl Gustavovich adopt?

6 Which four allied powers fought against Russia in the Crimean War?

7 What is the name of the student who commits murder in the novel *Crime and Punishment*?

8 Which scientific law states that the current in an electrical circuit equals its voltage divided by its resistance?

9 In which British city did the Peterloo Massacre of campaigners for parliamentary reform take place?

10 Which writer was offered the post of Poet Laureate in 1895 but turned it down?

11 What name was given to the formal declaration that the USA would not interfere in the affairs of Europe if Europe ceased its colonial ambitions in the western hemisphere?

12 Which socialist organisation was founded in 1884, taking its name from a cautious Roman General?

13 Who wrote: 'My love's like a red, red, rose that's newly sprung in June'?

14 Which European power colonized the country now known as Guinea-Bissau?

15 Who wrote *The Pied Piper of Hamelin*?

16 Which two famous Sioux chiefs defeated Custer at Little Bighorn?

17 The title of which famous novel contains a Yorkshire term for turbulent weather?

18 Who died a recluse in Chelsea, leaving 300 oil paintings, and over 20,000 water colours and drawings to Britain?

19 Which code became the basis of the French legal system in 1804?

20 What are the titles of the two novels by Anne Brontë?

1   The Lumière brothers

2   Benjamin Disraeli

3   Paul Gauguin

4   Walter Scott

5   Peter Carl Fabergé

6   Britain, France, Turkey and Sardinia

7   Raskolnikov

8   Ohm's law

9   Manchester, in 1819

10 Rudyard Kipling

11 The Monroe Doctrine of 1823

12 Fabian Society, named after Fabius Maximus

13 Robert Burns

14 Portugal (Portuguese Guinea)

15 Robert Browning

16 Crazy Horse and Sitting Bull

17 Wuthering Heights

18 J.M.W. Turner

19 Code Napoléon, or Civil Code

20 Agnes Grey and The Tenant of Wildfell Hall

1   Which fast Bohemian dance in double time became all the rage in 19th-century Europe?

2   Sir Robert Peel cut the number of capital offences in Britain from 200 to which four?

3   Which novel by William Makepeace Thackeray is subtitled 'a novel without a hero'?

4   Who was elected MP for Meath in 1875 and spent his life fighting for Irish Home Rule?

5   Which painting gave rise to the term Impressionism?

6   Which earldom was created for Disraeli in 1876?

7   Who wrote the novel *Daniel Deronda*?

8   Who was the last emperor of France?

9   Who composed the operas *Eugene Onegin* and *The Queen of Spades*?

10 To which drug was Samuel Taylor Coleridge addicted?

11 How many symphonies did Tchaikovsky write?

12 Which Dickens novel begins: 'It was the best of times, it was the worst of times'?

13 Who led the Confederate army that surrendered to the Union army at Appomattox to end the American Civil War?

14 Which German physicist predicted the existence of radio waves in 1887?

15 What were the names of the Brontë sisters' curate father and dissipated brother?

16 Which five countries did Simón Bolívar liberate in South America?

17 Which two plays by Oscar Wilde have the word 'importance' in their titles?

18 Which British socialist founded the half-million-strong Grand National Consolidated Trades Union?

19 Which aristocrat put forward the idea of an absolute measure of temperature?

20 Which ancient city, now Hisarlik in Turkey, did the archaeologist Heinrich Schliemann discover the site of?

1 The polka

2 High treason; forgery of banknotes; murder; arson in the Royal dockyards

3 Vanity Fair

4 Charles Stewart Parnell

5 Impression, Sunrise, by Claude Monet, painted in 1872

6 1st Earl of Beaconsfield

7 George Eliot

8 Napoleon III (1852–70)

9 Tchaikovsky

10 Opium

11 Six

12 A Tale of Two Cities

13 Robert E. Lee

14 Heinrich Hertz

15 The Reverend Patrick Brontë and Branwell Brontë

16 Bolivia (formerly Upper Peru), Peru, Venezuela, Colombia and Ecuador

17 The Importance of Being Earnest, A Woman of No Importance

18 Robert Owen

19 Lord Kelvin, who introduced the kelvin scale

20 Troy

1   Which chess piece does Alice start off as in *Through the Looking Glass*?

2   Which 1899 composition by Elgar features one tune played in many different ways?

3   Who wrote *Phenomenology of Spirit*, *Encyclopaedia of the Philosophical Sciences* and *Philosophy of Rights*?

4   What is Madame Bovary's first name in the novel *Madame Bovary* by Gustav Flaubert?

5   What name is given to the useful protein molecules produced in the blood discovered by bacteriologists in 1890?

6   How does *The Strange Case of Dr Jekyll and Mr Hyde* end?

7   What name was given to the four-wheeled carriage that could be drawn by one horse, named after the aristocrat who designed it?

8   Who was Tsar of Russia when the Crimean war began?

9   Which technological improvement did Sir Charles Parsons introduce to ships in 1894?

10 What name is given to the series of novels by Anthony Trollope that includes *Can You Forgive Her* and *The Duke's Children*?

11 Which foreign secretary did war secretary Castlereagh fight in a duel?

12 Who designed and built the Suez Canal?

13 In which Grimm's fairy tale does a prince climb up a maiden's hair?

14 Which one-word term is sometimes used for Conservatives of the mid-19th century who supported free trade?

15 Which English poet was a Jesuit priest?

16 Who was the first Englishwoman to receive a licence to practise medicine?

17 What is the name of the island to which jailed hero Edmond Dantes escapes in the novel *The Count of Monte Cristo*?

18 Which peninsula, later developed as a coaling stop for ships travelling from Suez, did Turkey give Britain in 1839?

19 What was Thomas Hardy's tragic last novel?

20 Louis Pasteur once said that in the field of observation, chance favours only the...what?

1   *White pawn*

2   *Enigma Variations*

3   *G.F.W. Hegel*

4   *Emma*

5   *Antibodies*

6   *Dr Jekyll commits suicide*

7   *A brougham, named after Lord Brougham*

8   *Nicholas I (1825–55)*

9   *The steam turbine*

10 *Palliser novels*

11 *George Canning*

12 *Ferdinand de Lesseps*

13 *Rapunzel*

14 *Peelites*

15 *Gerard Manley Hopkins*

16 *Elizabeth Garrett Anderson, in 1865*

17 *Monte Cristo*

18   *Aden*

19 *Jude the Obscure, 1896*

20 *Prepared mind*

1   Which was the last of Queen Victoria's jubilees?

2   Which 11-year-old pianist and composer took Vienna by storm in 1822?

3   Which issue caused a bitter rift in the Conservative party in the 1840s from which it took years to recover?

4   What was the first name of W. Somerset Maugham, born in 1874?

5   Who ordered the Charge of the Light Brigade?

6   Of which international company, originally dominated by France, did Britain purchase 40 per cent of the shares in 1875, making it the biggest single shareholder?

7   Which disputed works of art were bought for the British nation for £35,000?

8   Which worldwide organisation with over 20 million members was founded by George Williams in 1844?

9   Which famous French poet wrote most of his work before the age of 20?

10 During which war did the British army adopt khaki uniforms?

11 What is the name of the theatre set up by composer Richard Wagner at Bayreuth for performances of his works?

12 How are the fictional relatives Dimitri, Ivan and Alexei better known?

13 Which major war did the Ems Telegram spark off in 1870?

14 Which American poet said: 'The United States themselves are essentially the greatest poem'?

15 What name was given to the fortifications built on the southern coast of Britain against possible invasion by Napoleon?

16 Which writer spent hours in search of 'le mot juste' to perfect his sentences?

17 Who introduced the use of antiseptics in surgery?

18 Who wrote *The English Constitution*?

19 Under which royal House did Italy become a unified kingdom?

20 Which Derbyshire MP made sea travel safer?

1   *Her diamond jubilee, in 1897*

2   *Franz Liszt*

3   *Free trade (Corn Laws)*

4   *William*

5   *Lord Raglan made the original order which was misunderstood by Lord Lucan*

6   *The Suez Canal Company*

7   *The Elgin Marbles*

8   *The YMCA*

9   *Arthur Rimbaud*

10   *The South African War against the Boers*

11   *Festspielhaus (Festival playhouse)*

12   *As the Brothers Karamazov in the novel by Dostoyevsky*

13   *The Franco-Prussian War*

14   *Walt Whitman*

15   *Martello towers*

16   *Gustave Flaubert*

17   *Joseph Lister, in 1865*

18   *Walter Bagehot, in 1864*

19   *House of Savoy*

20   *Samuel Plimsoll, originator of the 'Plimsoll' mark painted on the side of ships*

1   Which country was known as the 'Sick Man of Europe'?

2   Who throws the fictional archdeacon Claude Frollo to his death?

3   In which year was the United Kingdom of Great Britain and Ireland created by the Act of Union?

4   Who were the architects of the rebuilt Houses of Parliament?

5   What was writer George Eliot's real name?

6   Who was Tsar of Russia when Napoleon invaded in 1812?

7   Which Russian novel begins: 'All happy families resemble each other but each unhappy family is unhappy in its own way'?

8   Who billed his circus as 'The Greatest Show on Earth'?

9   Who founded sociology?

10 In which story did detective Sherlock Holmes first appear?

11 Which one-word term refers to the movement to unite Italy in the 19th century?

12 Which American magazine, founded in 1850, serialised works by Dickens, Thackeray and George Eliot?

13 Who was the first woman to receive the British Order of Merit?

14 Which composer wrote the *Dichterliebe* song cycles based on poems by Heinrich Heine?

15 Who were the rulers of Germany, Austria-Hungary and Russia that formed the Dreikaiserbund or 'League of Three Emperors' in 1873?

16 Which Wilkie Collins novel is about the disappearance of an enormous diamond?

17 Which belief became an official doctrine of the Roman Catholic church under Pope Pius IX in 1854?

18 What was the English title of Brillat-Savarin's gastronomy classic *La Physiologie du Goût*?

19 Which leader said: 'I governed Europe sometimes, Austria never'?

20 In what year did the Indian Mutiny begin?

1   Turkey

2   Quasimodo, in the Hunchback of Notre Dame

3   1801

4   Augustus Pugin and Charles Barry

5   Mary Anne (Marian) Evans

6   Alexander I

7   Anna Karenina

8   P.T. Barnum

9   Auguste Comte

10   A Study in Scarlet

11   Risorgimento (resurrection)

12   Harper's

13   Florence Nightingale

14   Robert Schumann

15   William I of Germany, Francis Joseph of Austria-Hungary and Alexander II of Russia

16   The Moonstone, 1868

17   Immaculate conception

18   The Physiology of Taste

19   Prince Metternich, foreign minister and chancellor of Austria

20   1857

1 Who were barred from sitting in Parliament from 1673 until 1829?

2 What is the name of the kindly old gentleman who adopts Oliver at the end of *Oliver Twist*?

3 Which king of France was overthrown in the revolution of 1848?

4 What are the names of the four sisters in the book *Little Women*?

5 What happened to Cuba and the Philippines in 1898?

6 Which French Impressionist painted *Crystal Palace* and *The Road to Sydenham*?

7 In which book does Captain Nemo skipper the *Nautilus*?

8 To the nearest four days, what was the speed record for crossing the Atlantic by paddle steamship set in 1838?

9 Which political party did Keir Hardie form in 1893?

10 Which nationality was the composer Sibelius?

11 Which outlaw wore a metal helmet?

12 Which philosopher and MP wrote the book *Subjection of Women*?

13 How did the poet Lord Byron die?

14 In which novel does gentle Prince Myshkin refuse to take offence at anything?

15 Which was the first asteroid to be discovered?

16 In which year was the Battle of Trafalgar fought?

17 Which of Beethoven's symphonie is called the *Eroica*?

18 Which prime minister abolished Rotten Boroughs and extended the franchise in 1832?

19 What nationality was Adolphe Sax, the inventor of the Saxophone?

20 What did the USA buy from France for $15 million in 1803?

1   *Roman Catholics*

2   *Mr Brownlow*

3   *Louis Philippe*

4   *Jo, Meg, Beth and Amy*

5   *Spain lost them in the Spanish-American War*

6   *Camille Pissarro*

7   *Twenty Thousand Leagues Under the Sea*

8   *18 days, 12 hours*

9   *Independent Labour Party*

10   *Finnish*

11   *Ned Kelly*

12   *John Stuart Mill*

13   *He caught a fever at Missolonghi in 1824 while helping Greek rebels in their war of independence*

14   *The Idiot, by Dostoyevsky*

15   *Ceres, in 1801 by G. Piazzi*

16   *1805*

17   *The Third*

18   *Earl Grey*

19   *Belgian*

20   *Louisiana*

1   Where do the Martians first invade in War of the Worlds?

2   Who composed the *Moonlight Sonata*?

3   Which non-fiction book published in 1859 was at one time outsold only by the Bible in Britain?

4   In which decade did Queen Victoria come to the throne?

5   Which law, named after a French physicist, states that the line integral of the magnetic field around an arbitrarily chosen path is proportional to the net electric current enclosed by the path?

6   Which political party did prime minister Gladstone represent?

7   Which American created the pre-Sherlock Holmes sleuth C. Auguste Dupin?

8   Who made the Great Trek?

9   Apart from Preston, which was the only English football team in the 19th century to win the 'double'?

10 Which Tchaikovsky opera was based on a novel in verse by Alexander Pushkin?

11 Why are the San Francisco 49ers so called?

12 Which self-determination Bill did the Commons reject in 1886, the Lords in 1893 – but a coalition government finally pass in the next century?

13 Which art critic wrote the long treatise *Modern Painters*?

14 Which revolutionary event ended with the massacre of 25,000 people by French troops in Paris?

15 In which decade was the world's first underground railway opened to the public?

16 In which Jane Austen novel does Mrs Bennet aim to marry off her five daughters?

17 Which petition was discredited after being signed by 'Pug-nose', 'Mr Punch' and 'Victoria Rex' among thousands of others?

18 Where in Africa did Stanley find Livingstone?

19 Which government was the Jameson Raid of 1895 an attempt to overthrow?

20 In which novel is Bathsheba Everdene loved by the young adventurer Sergeant Troy, and by farmers Gabriel Oak and William Boldwood?

19th Century

1 Woking

2 Beethoven

3 Mrs Beeton's Household Management

4 1830s (1837)

5 Ampère's law

6 The Liberals

7 Edgar Allan Poe

8 Thousands of Dutch (Boer) settlers in the 1830s to escape British rule in southern Africa

9 Aston Villa, in 1897

10 Eugene Onegin

11 After the 1849 Gold Rush

12 Home rule for Ireland

13 John Ruskin

14 The Paris Commune, 1871

15 1860s (1863), in London, linking Paddington and Farringdon

16 Pride and Prejudice

17 The Chartists' petition calling for universal suffrage

18 At Ujiji on Lake Tanganyika

19 The government of the Transvaal

20 Far from the Madding Crowd, by Thomas Hardy, 1874

1   What is the catchphrase of the Queen of Hearts in *Alice's Adventures in Wonderland*?

2   Who shocked the Commons by turning up in cloth cap and tweeds when he took his seat in 1892?

3   How was Queen Victoria related to King William IV, her predecessor?

4   What is the subtitle of Tchaikovsky's Symphony No. 6?

5   Who was appointed Surveyor General of Metropolitan Roads in 1827?

6   Which artist did the original illustrations for Charles Dickens' *Oliver Twist*?

7   Which scientist was given a house to live in by Queen Victoria?

8   Which children's opera features the Sand Man, the Dew Man and the terrible Crunch Witch?

9   At which battle did Nelson put a telescope to his blind eye?

10   Which poet drowned aged 29 when his boat was caught in a storm?

11   Which nation, formed from the principalities of Moldavia and Wallachia, gained its independence in 1878?

12   Who built the first tunnel under the Thames, connecting Wapping and Rotherhithe?

13   Who wrote the book of poetry *Flowers of Evil* or *Les Fleurs du Mal*?

14   What name is given to the period in British history that lasted from February 1811 until January 1820?

15   What was Napoleon's star sign?

16   What is the title of the book published by Engels in 1844 about English workers?

17   What is the full name of the Mormon church founded in the USA by Joseph Smith?

18   Carbon fibres were first used commercially by inventor Thomas Edison. To what purpose did he put them?

19   Which Keats poem ends: 'Beauty is truth, truth beauty, – that is all Ye know on earth, and all Ye need to know'?

20   Which was the world's first public railway?

1   'Off with his head!'

2   James Keir Hardie

3   He was her uncle

4   'Pathétique'

5   John McAdam

6   George Cruikshank

7   Michael Faraday

8   Hansel and Gretel, by Engelbert Humperdinck

9   Battle of Copenhagen, in 1801

10 Shelley, in 1822

11 Romania

12 Marc Isambard Brunel, father of Isambard Kingdom Brunel

13 Baudelaire

14 The Regency, when the Prince of Wales exercised sovereignty because of George III's madness

15 Leo

16 The Condition of the Working Classes in England

17 Church of Jesus Christ of Latter-Day Saints

18 As the filaments in his electric light bulbs

19 Ode on a Grecian Urn

20 The Stockton and Darlington, which opened in 1825

1 Which Squire sails with Jim Hawkins in *Treasure Island*?

2 The horrors of which battle inspired Jean Henri Dunant to found the Red Cross?

3 In which novel do Betsy Trotwood and the Peggotty family appear?

4 Which town did German troops besiege for four months and nine days in 1870-71?

5 Which composer visited Britain ten times and wrote an overture to *A Midsummer Night's Dream*?

6 What is the chemical term for aspirin, first marketed in 1899 by German chemist Felix Hoffman?

7 Shelley's poem *Adonais* was a lament on the death of which poet?

8 Whose rule in India did the India Act abolish in 1858?

9 Which artist and writer founded the Arts and Crafts movement, dedicated to producing simple but beautiful handmade goods?

10 Who sailed to the Galapagos islands on HMS *Beagle*?

11 Which prime minister introduced a system of elementary education in 1870?

12 Who is the heroine of *Middlemarch*, by George Eliot?

13 What was the name of the mass movement led by the free traders Richard Cobden and John Bright?

14 Which of Schubert's symphonies is known as *the Unfinished*?

15 Which city did Georges Haussmann rebuild?

16 Which statesman said: 'When I want to read a novel, I write one'?

17 Which social reformer stopped British children being sent down the mines?

18 Which group of people did Percy Bysshe Shelley describe as the 'unacknowledged legislators of the world'?

19 Which German monarch and patron of the composer Wagner drowned himself after being declared insane?

20 Of which anarchist leader was it said: "On the first day of a revolution he is a treasure; on the second he ought to be shot'?

1   Squire Trelawney

2   Solferino, in 1859

3   David Copperfield, by Charles Dickens

4   Paris

5   Mendelssohn

6   Acetylsalicylic acid

7   John Keats

8   The East India Company's

9   William Morris

10   Charles Darwin

11   Gladstone

12   Dorothea Brooke

13   The Anti Corn Law League

14   Symphony No.8 in B Minor

15   Paris, planning its boulevards, parks, new bridges and the Bois de Boulogne

16   Benjamin Disraeli

17   Lord Shaftesbury

18   Poets

19   Ludwig II of Bavaria

20   Mikhail Bakunin

1 Which novel is set in the year 802701, with society divided into the Morlock and Eloi classes?

2 Who were the four British sovereigns of the 19th century?

3 Which piece of 19th-century music was chosen to be the national anthem of Europe?

4 On observing which event, did the French general Pierre Bosquet remark: 'It is magnificent, but it is not war'?

5 Which architect of the Poor Law and the workhouse was knighted in 1889?

6 Which two towns, on either side of a river, united in 1872 to form a capital city?

7 Who was the headmaster of Rugby school whose regime was the basis for Tom Brown's Schooldays?

8 What was Prince Albert's official title?

9 Which failed experiment of 1887 paved the way for Einstein to work out the theory of relativity?

10 Which British prime minister was shot dead in the lobby of the House of Commons?

11 Who wrote in the poem *Rabbi Ben Ezra*: 'Grow old along with me! The best is yet to be'?

12 In which year was slavery abolished in the British Empire?

13 What is the name of the convict who turns out to be Pip's benefactor in *Great Expectations*?

14 Which was the largest work by the French sculptor Frédéric Auguste Bartholdi?

15 What are the names of the two moons of Mars, discovered in 1877?

16 Which poet wrote: 'Every moment dies a man/ Every moment one is born'?

17 Who set up the first express company to carry freight west of Buffalo?

18 Who was the first king of a united Italy, from 1861 to 1878?

19 How does Dorian Gray die in *The Picture of Dorian Gray* by Oscar Wilde?

20 Who died after being shot in the back by Bob Ford?

1   The Time Machine, *by HG Wells*

2   *George III (1760–1820), George IV (1820–30), William IV (1830–7), Victoria (1837–1901)*

3   Ode to Joy, *from Beethoven's Ninth Symphony*

4   *The Charge of the Light Brigade*

5   *Edwin Chadwick*

6   *Buda and Pest, forming Budapest*

7   *Thomas Arnold*

8   *Prince Consort*

9   *The Michelson-Morley experiment which failed to find changes in the speed of light when it traveled with and against the earth's motion*

10 *Spencer Perceval, in 1812*

11 *Robert Browning*

12 *1833*

13 *Abel Magwitch*

14 *The Statue of Liberty*

15 *Phobos and Deimos*

16 *Alfred Lord Tennyson*

17 *Henry Wells and William George Fargo, in 1844*

18 *Victor Emmanuel II*

19 *He stabs his portrait and is then found dead with a knife through his heart*

20 *The outlaw Jesse James, in 1882*

1   In which year was the Storming of the Bastille?

2   Dr Johnson once said that a cucumber should be well-sliced, dressed with pepper and vinegar... and then what?

3   Who was the second president of the United States?

4   Which actress was a massive hit in Thomas Southerne's *Fatal Marriage* at Drury Lane in 1782?

5   How old was Mozart when he died?

6   Which Swiss chemist began the manufacture of 'Seltzer Water' soda in 1790?

7   Which three countries partitioned Poland until it disappeared from the map?

8   Which painter was born in East Bergholt, Suffolk?

9   Which Tsar worked as a shipbuilder in London?

10 Which poet wrote Ode *to Joy*, set to music by Beethoven in his last symphony?

11 Who wrote *The Adventures of Peregrine Pickle* about a rascally young man with a penchant for practical jokes?

12 Whose library, bequeathed to the British nation, formed the nucleus of the British Museum?

13 Who is usually referred to as Britain's first prime minister?

14 Which organisation was founded at Newmarket in about 1750 and still exists?

15 Which Englishman's pamphlets influenced both the American and French Revolutions?

16 What does it say on Sir Christopher Wren's memorial tablet in St Paul's Cathedral?

17 Where was Moll Flanders born in the picaresque novel by Daniel Defoe?

18 Which Italian's experiments on frogs led to the invention of the electric cell?

19 Which was the 'foggy month' in the French Revolutionary Calendar?

20 Who was the first European to sight Alaska?

1   *1789*

2   *Thrown out*

3   *John Adams (1797–1801)*

4   *Sarah Siddons*

5   *35*

6   *Jacob Schweppe*

7   *Russia, Prussia and Austria (in 1772, 1793 and 1795)*

8   *John Constable*

9   *Peter the Great*

10   *Friedrich Schiller*

11   *Tobias Smollet*

12   *British physician Hans Sloane's*

13   *Sir Robert Walpole (1721–42)*

14   *The Jockey Club*

15   *Thomas Paine's*

16   *'If you seek his monument, look about you'*

17   *Newgate*

18   *Luigi Galvani's*

19   *Brumaire*

20   *Vitus Bering in 1741*

1   Who was king when Britain lost the American colonies?

2   Who published the *Cabinet Maker and Upholsterer's Drawing Book* in the 1790s?

3   What was the pirate Blackbeard's real name?

4   Which king of Prussia was a noted musician?

5   Which novelist founded the Bow Street Runners?

6   Which joint company did James Watt set up to manufacture his steam engines?

7   Which of the original United States was – and still is – the smallest?

8   Which Italian put forward a revolutionary cyclical view of history in the book *New Science?*

9   Which term did philosopher Edmund Burke coin to describe the British press?

10   Upon the adventures of which Scottish sailor is the novel *Robinson Crusoe* based?

11   Which country first developed the metric system?

12   Who was the first director of the Royal Academy of Music?

13   Which philosopher proposed: 'the greatest happiness for the greatest number' as the basis for any law?

14   Which European city had to be completely rebuilt after a massive earthquake in 1755?

15   Which rare whitish metal resembling bright steel was discovered by Martin Heinrich Klaproth in 1789?

16   To which city is highwayman Dick Turpin supposed to have ridden in a single night from London on the mare Black Bess?

17   Which famous wood-carver died in 1721?

18   Which German philosopher wrote the book *Critique of Pure Reason?*

19   Which was the first 'classic' English horse race, introduced in 1776?

20   Which scientist was Warden of the Royal Mint?

1   George III

2   Thomas Sheraton

3   Edward Teach

4   Frederick the Great

5   Henry Fielding

6   Boulton and Watt

7   Rhode Island

8   Giambattista Vico, in 1725

9   The 'fourth estate'

10   Alexander Selkirk

11   France

12   George Frederick Handel

13   Jeremy Bentham

14   Lisbon

15   Uranium

16   York

17   Grinling Giibbons

18   Immanuel Kant

19   The St Leger, run at Doncaster

20   Sir Isaac Newton

1 Who became prime minister at the age of 24?

2 Who were the four Industrial Revolution inventors responsible for the flying shuttle, spinning jenny, spinning frame and 'mule'?

3 In which Mozart opera does a statue come to life?

4 Which scientific law states that the volume of a given mass of gas at constant pressure is directly proportional to its absolute temperature?

5 What was the main kind of wood used by the furniture maker Thomas Chippendale?

6 Which poem by Alexander Pope is about the theft of hair?

7 Which work, published in 1755, made Samuel Johnson's reputation?

8 What caused the decline of the Shakers religious sect?

9 Which statesman, author and inventor was called 'the wisest American'?

10 Which Scottish heroine disguised Bonnie Prince Charlie as her maid as he escaped to France after defeat at Culloden?

11 Which art form did Dr Johnson describe as 'an extravagant and irrational entertainment'?

12 In which 1798 battle did Nelson destroy Napoleon's naval power in the Mediterranean?

13 Which English poet committed suicide aged 17?

14 Which English scientist worked out the weight of the Earth and discovered hydrogen?

15 Which country became a Danish colony in 1729?

16 Where was William Chambers' 165 ft high Chinese Pagoda built?

17 Which work, published in 1776, is said to have been the first British book to deal systematically with the issues of economics?

18 What was the literary dispute known as the 'Baconian Controversy' about?

19 Which Austrian composer wrote 104 symphonies?

20 Which French Revolutionary leader was stabbed in his bath?

1   William Pitt the Younger, in 1783

2   John Kay (flying shuttle); James Hargreaves (spinning jenny); Richard Arkwright (spinning frame); Samuel Crompton (Crompton's mule)

3   Don Giovanni

4   Charles's law

5   Mahogany

6   The Rape of the Lock

7   Dictionary of the English Language

8   Their vow of celibacy

9   Benjamin Franklin

10 Flora MacDonald

11 Opera

12 Battle of the Nile

13 Thomas Chatterton, in 1770

14 Henry Cavendish

15 Greenland

16 Kew Gardens

17 The Wealth of Nations, by Adam Smith

18 The authorship of Shakespeare's plays

19 Joseph Haydn

20 Jean Paul Marat in 1793, by Charlotte Corday

1 Who said: 'Qu' ils mangent de la brioche'?

2 What was the date of the American Declaration of Independence?

3 What were the earliest steam engines used for?

4 Which religious movement was inspired by a mystical experience by its founder in Aldersgate Street, London?

5 Who wrote the novel *Pamela*, said to be the first 'modern' English novel?

6 Which non-British philosopher did Dr Johnson describe as 'a very bad man'?

7 Which term is used to describe the laws of 1799 and 1800 which barred British workers from taking collective action?

8 In which town was Beethoven born?

9 What name was given to the now discredited theory that the shape of the skull determined the shape of the brain and hence human character?

10 Which French navigator has a plant and some Pacific islands named after him?

11 Which ruler established Russia's frontier on the coast of the Black Sea?

12 Who founded homeopathy?

13 Which political group ousted the Girondins to seize power during the French Revolution?

14 Which were the two main political groups in the USA when George Washington became president?

15 How did Clive of India die?

16 Which oratorio by Haydn contains the aria 'The heavens are telling the glory of God'?

17 What nationality was Marie Antoinette?

18 Who invented the cotton gin?

19 Which musical key forms part of the title of J.S. Bach's mass of 1749?

20 With which county is the potter Josiah Wedgwood associated?

1   Marie Antoinette

2   4 July 1776

3   Pumping water out of mines

4   Methodism, founded by John Wesley

5   Samuel Richardson

6   Jean-Jacques Rousseau

7   Combination Laws

8   Bonn

9   Phrenology

10   Louis de Bougainville

11   Catherine the Great

12   German physician Samuel Hahnemann

13   Jacobins

14   Federalists and Republicans (or Republican Democrats)

15   He committed suicide, in 1774

16   The Creation

17   Austrian

18   Eli Whitney, in 1793

19   Mass in B minor

20   Staffordshire

1   What is the name of the land of giants in *Gulliver's Travels*?

2   Who was British prime minister throughout the French Revolution?

3   Name one of the two women who fall in love with Macheath in the *Beggar's Opera*.

4   In which decade was oxygen first identified?

5   Which two poets collaborated on the acclaimed volume *Lyrical Ballads*, containing *The Rime of the Ancient Mariner* and *Tintern Abbey*?

6   By which name is the philosopher, dramatist and poet François Marie Arouet usually known?

7   Which flower did botanist Carolus Linnaeus name *Bellis perennis* when he laid down the rules for botanical nomenclature?

8   Over which empress's succession to the throne was the War of the Austrian Succession fought?

9   What is the title of William Hogarth's series of engravings depicting a young man's journey from the pleasure-houses of London to Bedlam?

10 What was the name of the American provisional government during the American War of Independence?

11 What were the first names of the composer C.P.E. Bach, the third son of J.S. Bach?

12 Which cardiac drug was pioneered in the 18th century?

13 According to the poet William Blake, where does the 'road of excess' lead?

14 Which British general lost the decisive battle of Yorktown in the American War of Independence?

15 What was first published as *Vox Stellarum*, (*The Voice of the Stars*), but is now published under a different name?

16 Which city was known as the 'Athens of the North'?

17 Who wrote *Rule Britannia*?

18 Which astronomer discovered the planet Uranus?

19 Which German philosopher argued that 'this is the best of all possible worlds'?

20 What is the origin of the terms Left and Right in politics?

1   Brobdingnag

2   Pitt the Younger

3   Polly Peachum and Lucy Lockit

4   1770s

5   Samuel Taylor Coleridge and William Wordsworth

6   Voltaire

7   The daisy

8   Empress Maria Theresa of Austria

9   A Rake's Progress

10 Continental Congress

11 Carl Philipp Emanuel

12 Digitalis

13 To the palace of wisdom

14 Lord Cornwallis

15 Old Moore's Almanac

16 Edinburgh

17 Thomas Augustine Arne

18 Sir William Herschel, in 1781

19 Leibniz

20 From the French Revolution. Those most in favour of radical change sat on the left in the National Assembly

1   Which duke defeated the Scots at the battle of Culloden in 1746?

2   Of which royal family was it said: 'They learned nothing and forgot nothing'?

3   Which party produced most of Britain's prime ministers in the 18th century?

4   Which set of six works did J.S. Bach publish in 1721?

5   What did Britain 'lose' between 3 September 1752 and 14 September 1752?

6   In which smash-hit comedy by the dramatist Sheridan did Lady Sneerwell run a salon for gossips?

7   Against which group were the Gordon Riots of 1780 directed?

8   What communication system did Claude Chappe invent in 1793?

9   What is the origin of the word Rococo?

10   The name of which Italian town is synonymous with the violins of Antonio Stradivari and Giuseppe Guarneri?

11   Which committee ruled France during the Reign of Terror?

12   Which poet and satirist wrote: 'A little learning is a dangerous thing'?

13   In which ship did Captain Cook first sail to the South Seas?

14   What was the name of Mozart's father and teacher?

15   In which capital city was the *Encyclopaedia Britannica* first published?

16   Who wrote *120 Days of Sodom*?

17   What was George III's nickname?

18   Which painter, who lived from 1712–93, is famous for his souvenir views of Venice?

19   Which Irishman became a Yorkshire vicar at the age of 25 and went on to create the comic anti-hero Tristram Shandy?

20   Who wrote *A Vindication of the Rights of Women*?

1   The Duke of Cumberland

2   The French Bourbons

3   The Whigs

4   Brandenburg Concertos

5   Eleven days, when under the newly adopted Gregorian calendar 3 September became 14 September

6   School for Scandal

7   Catholics

8   Semaphore

9   From the French 'rocaille'. meaning rock-work

10   Cremona

11   The Committee of Public Safety

12   Alexander Pope

13   Endeavour

14   Leopold Mozart

15   Edinburgh, in 1768

16   The Marquis de Sade

17   Farmer George

18   Francesco Guardi

19   Laurence Sterne

20   Mary Wollstonecraft

1 Which term refers to the golden age of English prose at the time of Swift and Pope?

2 Who first used mercury in a thermometer?

3 By which name is Mozart's Serenade K.525 usually known?

4 How did Voltaire sum up the Holy Roman Empire?

5 Who was appointed Astronomer Royal in 1720?

6 Which great portrait painter was the first president of the Royal Academy?

7 Which two European countries merged their parliaments in 1707?

8 Who pioneered vaccination using cowpox?

9 What burst in 1720 ruining thousands?

10 Who had six wives and was hanged at Tyburn for housebreaking?

11 What, on the continent, were known as 'English overcoats' or 'umbrellas'?

12 How did James Watt improve the steam engine?

13 Which brothers were chiefly responsible for the building of Edinburgh's New Town?

14 Which MP and favourite of the London mob died in 1797?

15 Which was the first European country to introduce compulsory elementary schooling?

16 Which French Rococo artist became court painter to Louis XV on the death of van Loo?

17 Which philosopher wrote: 'Man is born free, and everywhere he is in chains'?

18 What was the composer Vivaldi's first name?

19 Which 1759 Act of Parliament revolutionised transport?

20 Which explosive piece did Handel write for Londoners to celebrate the Peace of Aix-la-Chapelle?

1   Augustan Age

2   Daniel Fahrenheit

3   Eine kleine Nachtmusik

4   He said it was 'neither Holy, nor Roman, nor an Empire'

5   Edmund Halley

6   Sir Joshua Reynolds

7   England and Scotland

8   Edward Jenner

9   The South Sea Bubble

10   Jonathan Wild, in 1725

11   Condoms

12   He invented the separate condenser

13   John and Robert Adam

14   The radical political reformer John Wilkes

15   Prussia

16   François Boucher

17   Jean-Jacques Rousseau

18   Antonio

19   The Canal Act, which paved the way for a national network of canals

20   Music for the Royal Fireworks

1   Horace Walpole's *The Castle of Otranto* is said to be the first example of what kind of novel?

2   Which dramatist created the rascally hero Figaro in the plays *The Barber of Seville* and *The Marriage of Figaro*?

3   What was Robespierre's first name?

4   Which king bought Buckingham Palace?

5   Which term was coined in the 18th century to describe intellectual hostesses such as Mary Wortley Montagu and Mrs Mary Delany?

6   What is the popular name for Bonnie Prince Charlie's Jacobite rebellion of 1745?

7   Where did William Blake's 'Tyger! Tyger!' burn bright?

8   Which sport is associated with the Hambledon club?

9   What was the surname of Alessandro and Domenico, who died in 1725 and 1757 respectively?

10   Which 13-year war did Britain and her allies fight in a bid to stop Bourbons sitting on the Spanish throne?

11   Who introduced coke for smelting iron at his foundry at Coalbrookdale, Shropshire?

12   Who was prime minister when Britain lost the American colonies?

13   How many states signed the Declaration of Independence?

14   What is the title of Blackstone's commentaries on law?

15   Which English portrait- and landscape-artist painted the 1770 masterpiece *The Blue Boy*?

16   Which Frenchman first demonstrated that water consisted of oxygen and hydrogen?

7   Who is 'conquered' by Miss Hardcastle in Oliver Goldsmith's comedy *She Stoops to Conquer*?

8   Who was George IV's 'secret' wife?

9   Who wrote the poem *Elegy Written in a Country Churchyard*?

0   Who developed a practical steam-powered engine in 1712?

1   *Gothic*

2   *Beaumarchais*

3   *Maximilien*

4   *George III*

5   *Bluestockings*

6   *The Forty-Five*

7   *In the forests of the night*

8   *Cricket*

9   *Scarlatti*

10   *The War of the Spanish Succession*

11   *Abraham Darby*

12   *Lord North*

13   *13*

14   *Commentaries*

15   *Thomas Gainsborough*

16   *Antoine Lavoisier*

17   *Marlowe*

18   *Maria Fitzherbert whom he married illegally in 1785*

19   *Thomas Gray*

20   *Thomas Newcomen*

18th Century

1 For which king did Handel write his *Water Music*?

2 Which Squire is Tom Jones's foster father in the novel by Henry Fielding?

3 Which 1730 invention lowered the price of crops?

4 Which satirist said: 'We have just enough religion to make us hate, but not enough to make us love one another'?

5 Which general won the Battle of Quebec to establish British control of Canada?

6 Who died in the Bastille in 1703 after more than 40 years behind bars?

7 Which plant specimens did William Bligh voyage to the Pacific in the *Bounty* to collect?

8 Which national newspaper was founded in 1791 and is still known by the same name?

9 Who invented the piano?

10 Who wrote *An Essay on Population*?

11 Whose mistress was Madame de Pompadour?

12 Which famous opera has the English title: 'Women are all the same'?

13 On which historic 1776 document is it written: 'Governments derive their just powers from the consent of the governed'?

14 Which Jacobite is immortalised in the title of a novel by Sir Walter Scott?

15 Which family employed the composer Haydn for more than three decades?

16 Who first described England as a 'nation of shopkeepers'?

17 What disguise did the US colonists adopt when they threw tea into Boston harbour during the Boston Tea Party?

18 What is the title of historian Edward Gibbon's masterpiece?

19 Who sent up a cock, a duck and a sheep in a hot air balloon?

20 What did the Recusants of the 17th and 18th centuries refuse to do in Britain?

1   George I

2   Squire Allworthy

3   Jethro Tull's seed drill

4   Jonathan Swift

5   General James Wolfe, who died during the battle on 13 September 1759

6   The Man in the Iron Mask

7   Breadfruit

8   The Observer

9   Bartolomeo Cristofori, c.1709

10   Thomas Malthus, in 1798

11   Louis XV's

12   Mozart's Cosi fan Tutte

13   The American Declaration of Independence

14   Rob Roy

15   The Esterhazy family

16   The economist Adam Smith, in The Wealth of Nations

17   They dressed as Indians

18   The History of the Decline and Fall of the Roman Empire

19   The Montgolfier brothers in a demonstration of their balloon for Louis XVI at the Palace of Versailles in 1783

20   Attend the services of the Church of England

1   Who said: 'She is as headstrong as an allegory on the banks of the Nile'?

2   In which architectural style is the White House built?

3   Which countries fought a war over an ear?

4   Who were the two compilers of the 33-volume *Encyclopédie*?

5   What was Rob Roy's real name?

6   What did the city of Meissen become famous for?

7   What was *The Times* newspaper called when it was founded in 1785?

8   Which ruling body did Napoleon overthrow to seize power in France?

9   Agriculturist Viscount Townshend pioneered crop rotation and winter feed for cattle. What was his nickname?

10 Who had 17 children while married to Prince George of Denmark, of which only one survived?

11 Which extant magazine was founded by Richard Steele and Joseph Addison?

12 Which Hindu goddess of destruction did the Thugs sect in India worship?

13 Who lived at 17 Gough Square from 1748–59?

14 Which poet wrote the hymn: 'God moves in a Mysterious way, His Wonders to Perform'?

15 Which general fought the British in the American Revolution and sat in the National Assembly in France during the French Revolution?

16 Who was the last monarch to live at Hampton Court?

17 Lord Lovat was the last person to be beheaded in England. What was his crime?

18 Which bishop and philosopher argued that reality consisted of ideas in the mind of God?

19 Which revolutionary song did army officer Claude Joseph Rouget de Lisle write?

20 With which city is the painter Canaletto associated apart from Venice?

1   *Mrs Malaprop in Sheridan's* The Rivals

2   *Neo-Classical*

3   *Britain and Spain in the War of Jenkin's Ear (1739–41)*

4   *D'Alembert and Diderot*

5   *Robert MacGregor*

6   *Porcelain*

7   **The Daily Universal Register**

8   *The Directory, in 1799*

9   *'Turnip' Townshend*

10   *Queen Anne of Great Britain and Ireland*

11   **The Spectator**

12   *Kali*

13   *Samuel Johnson*

14   *William Cowper*

15   *Marquis de Lafayette*

16   *George II*

17   *He took part in the Jacobite uprising of 1745*

18   *Bishop George Berkeley*

19   **La Marseillaise**

20   *London, where he spent ten years (1746–55)*

1   Who was king of England at the time of the Great Fire of London?

2   Which subject did Francis Bacon call 'that great mother of the sciences'?

3   Who kills Laertes and Claudius during Hamlet's death scene?

4   Which tavern in Cheapside, London was a meeting place for the likes of Ben Johnson, Sir Walter Raleigh, Shakespeare and many other celebrated early 17th-century figures?

5   How many standard laws of motion did Sir Isaac Newton develop?

6   Which three major composers were born in 1685?

7   Which English explorer gave his name to a river, a bay and a strait and died in 1611?

8   What strongly flavoured cheese did Samuel Pepys bury in his garden during the Great Fire?

9   Who says in the 'barge' scene in Antony and Cleopatra: 'Age cannot wither her, nor custom stale her infinite variety'?

10 In 1682 the explorer Robert La Salle became the first European to travel down which 2,350-mile river to which gulf?

11 What was founded by Act of Parliament in 1694 to help finance a war in Europe?

12 In which decade did the Pilgrim Fathers set sail for America in the Mayflower?

13 Which British king succeeded James I?

14 Which Dutch philosopher earned his living as a lens grinder?

15 Who was the military leader of the Pilgrim Fathers' colony at Plymouth, Massachusetts?

16 What was the title of Izaak Walton's treatise on fishing?

17 Who became chief minister of France in 1624?

18 Which company's main base was at one time Batavia in Java?

19 Which is the oldest university in the USA?

20 Who wrote the poem *Hudibras*, poking fun at the Puritans?

*C*17th*entury*

1 Charles II

2 Philosophy

3 Hamlet

4 The Mermaid, Bread Street

5 Three

6 Bach, Handel and Domenico Scarlatti

7 Henry Hudson

8 A parmesan

9 Enobarbus

10 The Mississippi River to the Gulf of Mexico

11 The Bank of England

12 1620s (1620)

13 Charles I, in 1625

14 Benedict Spinoza

15 Myles Standish

16 The Compleat Angler

17 Cardinal Richelieu

18 Dutch East India Company

19 Harvard, founded in 1636

20 Samuel Butler

1   Which was the first battle of the English Civil War?

2   Where was the dodo found until it was eaten to extinction by settlers?

3   Who was king of England at the time of the Gunpowder Plot?

4   Who discovered that the volume of a given mass of gas at a constant temperature is inversely proportional to its pressure?

5   Who married John Rolfe and died on board ship near Gravesend?

6   Which French king was a keen ballet dancer?

7   What did the Dutch buy from Algonquin Indians in 1626?

8   Which dramatist wrote the tragedies *The White Devil* and *The Duchess of Malfi*?

9   Which Civil War general fought for the Royalists, joined the Roundheads and was finally a major architect of the Restoration?

10 What follows the line: 'I come to bury Caesar, not to praise him'?

11 Which Flemish artist was knighted by Charles I?

12 Which Tsar founded the Romanov dynasty?

13 Which Mogul emperor built the Taj Mahal for his wife Mumtaz?

14 Who was the first official Poet Laureate and the author of the tragi-comedy *Marriage à la Mode*?

15 Which king was surrounded by a corrupt clique of ministers known from their initials as the Cabal?

16 Which English scientist discovered the circulation of the blood?

17 Which national theatre company was founded by Louis XIV of France?

18 Who became Britain's sovereigns in the Glorious Revolution?

19 Who says: 'Oh, brave new world, that has such people in it'?

20 Which learned institution originated in 1645 and was chartered in 1662?

1   The Battle of Edgehill, Warwickshire, 1642

2   Mauritius

3   James I

4   Robert Boyle

5   Pocahontas

6   Louis XIV

7   Manhattan

8   John Webster

9   General George Monck, Duke of Albermarle

10 'The evil that men do lives after them, The good is oft interred with their bones'

11 Sir Anthony Van Dyck

12 Tsar Michael (1613–45)

13 Shah Jahan

14 John Dryden

15 Charles II

16 William Harvey

17 Comédie-Francaise, established in 1680

18 William III (William of Orange) and Mary

19 Miranda, in The Tempest

20 The Royal Society

1   Which London theatre first opened in 1663?

2   Which Englishman built the world's first working steam engine?

3   Which writer spent more than 10 years in Bedford jail for preaching without a license?

4   In which year did Charles I lose his head?

5   Which Italian wrote the operas *Orfeo*, *The Legend of Orpheus* and *The Coronation of Poppea*?

6   Who was Witchfinder General during the English Civil War?

7   Who wrote the book *De Jure Belli et Pacis* (*On the Law of War and Peace*), which founded international law?

8   What began in 1618 as a religious conflict and ended in 1648 with the Peace of Westphalia?

9   Which German astronomer first proved that planetary orbits are elliptical?

10 Which architect's two best-known buildings are the Queen's House, Greenwich, and the Banqueting Hall in Whitehall?

11 Who fabricated the Popish Plot, falsely claiming that Catholics planned to kill Charles II?

12 What was the dramatist Molière's real name?

13 What did the Dutch water-engineer Cornelius Vermuyden do in eastern England in 1634?

14 Which king planted Ulster with Protestant settlers from England and Scotland?

15 Which English philosopher wrote *An Essay Concerning Human Understanding* and helped found empiricism?

16 Which shogunate ruled Japan from 1603 until 1868?

17 Which king fled to France after William of Orange was offered the British throne?

18 Which 17th-century mathematical theorem remained unproven until the 20th century?

19 Which Swedish king and hero of the Thirty Years War is said to have been one of the greatest generals the world has ever seen?

20 Who painted himself more than 100 times?

1   *Drury Lane*

2   *Thomas Savery, in 1696*

3   *John Bunyan*

4   *1649*

5   *Claudio Monteverdi*

6   *Matthew Hopkins*

7   *Hugo Grotius*

8   *The Thirty Years War*

9   *Johannes Kepler*

10   *Inigo Jones*

11   *Titus Oates, in 1678*

12   *Jean Baptiste Poquelin*

13   *He drained the Fens for the Duke of Bedford*

14   *James I*

15   *John Locke in 1690*

16   *The Tokugawa*

17   *James II*

18   *Fermat's Last Theorem – finally proved by Andrew Wiles of Princeton University in 1993–4*

19   *Gustavus Adolphus*

20   *Rembrandt*

1   Who was the first Englishwoman to earn a living by writing?

2   What name is given to the 1689 document that established Parliament as Britain's primary governing body?

3   Which knighted Dutch portraitist painted Oliver Cromwell 'warts and all'?

4   What is the French translation of Louis XIV's remark: 'I am the State'?

5   Who conducted the Bloody Assizes?

6   What begins: 'Of Man's first disobedience and the fruit'?

7   What nickname was given to the Parliament that executed Charles I?

8   Who invented the telescope?

9   At which battle did Oliver Cromwell earn the nickname Ironsides?

10 Which society did Cardinal Richelieu found in 1635 to preserve the purity of French?

11 In which poem would you find the lines: 'But at my back I always hear, Time's winged chariot hurrying near'?

12 Which German and which Englishman were jointly but separately responsible for the invention of calculus?

13 Which country colonised Curaçao in 1634?

14 Which illegitimate son of Charles II led a rebellion against his uncle James II?

15 Which baroque composer provided the music for the funeral of Queen Mary and is buried beneath the organ in Westminster Abbey?

16 Who sailed to America in 1681 to found a colony for oppressed Quakers?

17 Who created the Fountain of the Four Rivers in Rome?

18 The 'Red Duster' was authorized in 1674. What is it?

19 Who was the last Dutch governor of New Amsterdam before it became New York?

20 What name is given to a triangular formation of numbers in which each number is equal to the sum of the two numbers above it?

1 Aphra Behn

2 The Bill of Rights

3 Sir Peter Lely

4 L'État c'est moi

5 Judge Jeffreys

6 Paradise Lost, by John Milton

7 Rump Parliament

8 The Dutchman Hans Lippershey

9 Marston Moor in 1644

10 Académie Francaise

11 To His Coy Mistress, by Andrew Marvell

12 Leibniz and Newton

13 Holland

14 The Duke of Monmouth

15 Henry Purcell

16 William Penn, who founded Pennsylvania

17 Bernini, between 1648 and 1651

18 The nickname for the flag of the Merchant Navy

19 Peter Stuyvesant

20 Pascal's triangle

1   Whose mistress was the actress Nell Gwynn?

2   What was Samuel Pepys' job?

3   What is the subtitle of Ben Jonson's play *Volpone*?

4   Which was the decisive battle of the English Civil War in which the Roundheads defeated the Royalists on 14 June 1645?

5   Which English philosopher claimed that life without an absolute form of government would be 'nasty, brutish and short'?

6   In which town in South Holland did the Dutch artist Vermeer live and work?

7   Which branch of mathematics was invented by the Scot John Napier?

8   Which architect built the first properly Classical buildings in England?

9   Who was the queen of Charles II, responsible for the introduction of tea-drinking to England?

10   Who tried to steal the Crown Jewels?

11   What event do Orange Order marches through Catholic areas of Ulster celebrate each July?

12   In which Shakespeare play would you find the characters Leontes, Hermione and Polixenes?

13   Which Dutch scientist and pioneer of the microscope was the first man to observe and describe red blood cells and bacteria?

14   In which Amsterdam museum can you see Rembrandt's *Parade of the Civic Guard under Captain Frans Banning Cocq*?

15   Which monarch had Sir Walter Raleigh executed?

16   Which 17th-century philosopher, politician and writer has the same name as a famous 20th-century painter?

17   Which English composer, renowned for his church music and madrigals, was appointed organist at Westminster Abbey in 1623?

18   Who wrote the plays *The Fatal Marriage* and *Oroonoko*, based on novels by Mrs Aphra Behn?

19   What name is given to the republic set up in 1649 after the execution of Charles I?

20   Which European capital city did the Polish King John III rescue from the Turks after they had besieged it in 1683?

C*17th*
Century

1 *Charles II's*

2 *Secretary to the Admiralty*

3 *The Fox*

4 *The Battle of Naseby*

5 *Thomas Hobbes*

6 *Delft*

7 *Logarithms*

8 *Inigo Jones*

9 *Catherine of Braganza*

10 *'Captain' Thomas Blood*

11 *The defeat of the Catholic James II by William III (of Orange) at the Battle of the Boyne in 1690*

12 *The Winter's Tale*

13 *Anton van Leeuwenhoek*

14 *Rijksmuseum*

15 *James I, in 1618*

16 *Francis Bacon*

17 *Orlando Gibbons*

18 *Thomas Southerne*

19 *The Commonwealth*

20 *Vienna*

1 Who is the pilgrim hero of John Bunyan's *Pilgrim's Progress*?

2 What was Oliver Cromwell's title from 1653 until his death?

3 Which work, published in 1687 by Sir Isaac Newton, has been called 'the greatest single work of science in the world'?

4 What was ironic about the death of the dramatist Molière?

5 Who said: 'I think therefore I am'?

6 Which of Shakespeare's characters delivers the line: 'Who steals my purse steals trash'?

7 Where was Charles I beheaded?

8 Which branch of warfare did the French marshal and military engineer Sebastién Vauban revolutionise?

9 Which school of poetry did John Donne found?

10 What was chartered in 1670 to develop northern Canada?

11 Which pirate was knighted and made Lieutenant Governor of Jamaica?

12 Which Milton play climaxes with the destruction of a temple?

13 Who were the seven British sovereigns of the 17th century?

14 Which country was barred to foreigners from 1639 until the middle of the 19th century?

15 Which Oxford theatre was designed by Sir Christopher Wren?

16 Which Spanish sea captain gave his name to a strait after sailing between Australia and New Guinea?

17 Which astronomer founded the Royal Observatory at Greenwich?

18 Who designed Blenheim Palace and Castle Howard as well as writing comic plays?

19 In which city is North America's oldest university, Laval?

20 What was the year of the Great Fire of London?

1   Christian

2   Lord Protector of the Commonwealth

3   Principia

4   He collapsed on stage while playing the part of a hypochondriac in one of his own plays and died the same day

5   René Descartes

6   Iago in Othello

7   Outside the Banqueting House, Whitehall

8   Siege warfare

9   Metaphysical

10 The Hudson Bay Company

11 Sir Henry Morgan

12 Samson Agonistes

13 Elizabeth I (1558–1603), James I (1603–25), Charles I (1625–49), Charles II (1660–85), James II (1685–8), William III (1689–1702) and Mary (1689–94)

14 Japan

15 The Sheldonian Theatre

16 Luis de Torres

17 John Flamsteed, in 1675

18 Sir John Vanbrugh

19 Québec

20 1666

1   What was Charles II's nickname?

2   Which poet was dubbed 'the Wicked Earl'?

3   What is the 'age' that followed the Elizabethan called?

4   Which epic poem, published in four books in 1671, deals with the temptation of Christ in the Wilderness?

5   In which American colony did the Salem witch trials take place?

6   Which of the planets were known to man in the 17th century?

7   Who is the thane of Fife in Shakespeare's *Macbeth*?

8   Which Dutch university set up the world's first chemistry lab?

9   Which Roman Catholic movement was launched at the Council of Trent in 1545 and lasted into the 17th century?

10   Which major art form was founded in the early 17th century?

11   What was dug up and hung at Tyburn on 30 January 1661?

12   Where was the first permanent English colony in America?

13   Who was the father of the first duke of Marlborough?

14   To whom were Shakespeare's sonnets dedicated?

15   Which mathematical instrument did Englishman William Oughtred invent?

16   Which prince lost the battles of Marston Moor and Naseby in the English Civil War?

17   Where would you find the allegorical City of Destruction, Celestial City, Help and the Slough of Despond?

18   Which Dutch colonial administrator founded Cape Town?

19   Who designed the gardens at Versailles?

20   After which Dutch governor general of the East Indies was Tasmania originally named?

1   The Merry Monarch

2   John Wilmot, Earl of Rochester

3   Jacobean

4   Paradise Regained, by John Milton

5   Massachusetts, in 1692

6   Mercury, Venus, Mars, Jupiter, Saturn (and Earth)

7   Macduff

8   Leyden University

9   The Counter Reformation

10   Opera

11   The body of Oliver Cromwell

12   Jamestown, Virginia, established in 1607

13   Sir Winston Churchill

14   'Mr W.H.'

15   The slide rule

16   Prince Rupert

17   In John Bunyan's Pilgrim's Progress

18   Jan van Riebeeck, in 1652

19   André Le Nôtre

20   Anthony Van Dieman

1 Which king united the English and Scottish crowns?

2 What does the 'green eyed monster' mock, according to Shakespeare?

3 Which painter was forced to flee Rome after killing a man in a brawl?

4 Which gas was first discovered by JB van Helmont in 1630?

5 Who wrote the banned masterpiece *Dialogue on the Two Chief World Systems*?

6 Which philosophical doctrine is founded on Descartes' 'I think, therefore I am' proposition?

7 Which English politician was known as 'the Trimmer'?

8 In which year did Queen Elizabeth I die?

9 Which book, first published in 1549, was revised at various times until its form was established by an Act of Parliament in 1662?

10 Which means of transport did Dutch engineer Cornelius Drebbel pioneer in 1620?

11 What are the names of King Lear's daughters?

12 Who was Tumbledown Dick?

13 What are the names of Don Quixote's horse and his faithful manservant?

14 What were Charles II's last words?

15 Which Italian composer, born in 1653, had the first name Arcangelo?

16 In which London museum can you see the *Laughing Cavalier*?

17 In which allegorical satire do the brothers Peter, Jack and Martin represent the Roman Catholic, extreme Protestant and Anglican churches?

18 Which Flemish master painted *Paris Awards the Golden Apple to Venus*?

19 In which church is Shakespeare buried?

20 Which printmaking technique, which depends on the fact that grease and water do not mix, was invented by the German Alois Senefelder?

1   James I (James VI of Scotland), by his accession to the English throne in 1603

2   The meat it feeds on

3   Caravaggio

4   Carbon dioxide

5   Galileo

6   Dualism

7   George Savile, 1st Marquis of Halifax

8   1603

9   The Book of Common Prayer

10 The submarine

11 Cordelia, Goneril and Regan

12 Richard Cromwell, who succeeded his father Oliver Cromwell as Lord Protector in 1658

13 Rozinante and Sancho Panza

14 'Let not poor Nellie starve'

15 Corelli

16 The Wallace Collection

17 Tale of a Tub, by Jonathan Swift

18 Peter Paul Rubens

19 Holy Trinity Church, Stratford-on-Avon

20 Lithography

1 Where did Martin Luther nail his 95 Theses?

2 Which painter was born in Crete and died in Toledo?

3 Who met whom on the Field of the Cloth of Gold?

4 What blesses 'him that gives and him that takes', according to Shakespeare?

5 What name was given to the annual Papal levy of a penny, paid by many English households?

6 What did Machiavelli say should be 'the only study of a prince'?

7 Which of his wives did Henry VIII divorce apart from Catherine of Aragon?

8 Who commanded the Spanish Armada?

9 Name three of the five Shakespeare plays in which there is a character called Antonio?

10 Who was called 'the master-thief of the unknown world'?

11 Which butcher's son became one of the richest men in England?

12 Who was lecturer in maths at Pisa university in the 1580s?

13 With which city do you associate the painter Titian?

14 Who was executed in 1535 and canonized in 1935?

15 Who were massacred in the Saint Bartholomew's Day Massacre?

16 Which 16th-century composer inspired a modern composer to write a much-loved Fantasia?

17 What name is given to the Yorkshire and Lincolnshire rebellions against Henry VIII in the 1530s?

18 Which style of painting, characterised by distortions and elongations of the human figure, succeeded High Renaissance?

19 Which city did Ivan the Terrible capture from the Tatars in 1552?

20 Which bishop of London was burned as a heretic by Bloody Mary?

1   On a church door in Wittenberg

2   El Greco

3   Henry VIII met Francis I of France in 1520

4   'The quality of mercy'

5   Peter's pence

6   War

7   Anne of Cleves

8   The Duke of Medina Sidonia

9   The Merchant of Venice, The Tempest, Two Gentlemen of Verona, Much Ado About Nothing and Twelfth Night

10   Francis Drake

11   Cardinal Wolsey

12   Galileo

13   Venice

14   Sir Thomas More

15   Huguenots or French Protestants, in France on 24 August 1572

16   Thomas Tallis, who inspired Fantasia on a Theme by Thomas Tallis, by Vaughan Williams

17   The Pilgrimage of Grace

18   Mannerism

19   Kazan

20   Nicholas Ridley, in 1555

1 For which Pope did Michelangelo paint the ceiling of the Sistine Chapel?

2 In which epic poem is Gloriana the Queen of Faeryland?

3 Who was the first English slave trader?

4 Who translated the Bible into English but was then burned as a heretic in Belgium?

5 How many lines are there in a sonnet?

6 Which Italian composer, who died in 1594, is said to have been the greatest master of Renaissance counterpoint?

7 Which Holy Roman Emperor said: 'I speak Spanish to God, Italian to women, French to men and German to my horse'?

8 In which comedy does Ferdinand, king of Navarre, take an oath to give up the company of women?

9 Who founded the Jesuits?

10 Who defeated the Sultan of Delhi to found the Mogul Empire?

11 Which dramatist was killed in a tavern brawl?

12 Who founded the Church of Scotland?

13 Which city did Warsaw replace as capital of Poland?

14 Which English possession did Queen Mary lose in 1558?

15 Portugal's national epic poem The Lusiads is about whose exploits?

16 For how long was Lady Jane Grey queen of England?

17 In which city is Romeo and Juliet set?

18 Who set up a theocracy in Geneva?

19 Apart from his works as a sculptor and goldsmith, what did Benevenuto Cellini leave to posterity?

20 Who was the architect of Henry VIII's break with Rome, who was executed in 1540 for treason?

1   *Julius II*

2   *The Faerie Queene, by Edmund Spenser*

3   *Admiral Sir John Hawkins*

4   *William Tyndale*

5   *14*

6   *Giovanni da Palestrina*

7   *Charles V*

8   *Love's Labour's Lost*

9   *St Ignatius Loyola*

10   *Babur, at the Battle of Panipat (1526)*

11   *Christopher Marlowe, in 1593*

12   *John Knox*

13   *Krakow*

14   *Calais*

15   *Explorer Vasco da Gama*

16   *Nine days*

17   *Verona*

18   *John Calvin*

19   *His autobiography*

20   *Thomas Cromwell*

1 What is the first line of *Twelfth Night*?

2 Which legendary ruler coated his body in gold dust?

3 What is the title of the book of doom-laden visions by Nostradamus?

4 Which High Renaissance painter died in 1520 aged 37?

5 At which battle was King James IV of Scotland killed?

6 Which Aztec capital did Hernando Cortés conquer?

7 Which Lord Chancellor resigned in protest after Henry VIII declared himself head of the church?

8 Who said: 'May God be my witness that there will not be a poor man in my Tsardom'?

9 In which western European city is there a mosque that houses a 16th-century cathedral?

10 Which Elizabethan soldier and navigator was Sir Walter Raleigh's half-brother?

11 Who wrote *Gargantua* and *Pantagruel* and gave his name to an adjective?

12 To which favourite did Queen Elizabeth give a castle at Kenilworth?

13 Which Tsar killed his son in a fit of rage?

14 Which Spanish king married Queen Mary I of England?

15 Which Italian painter and architect is best known for his biographies of other artists?

16 Which city, founded in 1577, is the holy city of Sikhism?

17 Which German-born artist, who died in 1543, was court painter to Henry VIII?

18 Which island did the Turks capture from the Venetians in the late 16th century and keep until the First World War?

19 Which explorer laid down the French claim to Canada?

20 Which English dramatist killed a man in a duel?

1   'If music be the food of love, play on.'

2   El Dorado

3   Centuries

4   Raphael

5   The Battle of Flodden, Northumberland, 1513

6   Tenochtitlan

7   Sir Thomas More

8   Boris Godunov, at his coronation in 1598

9   Cordoba

10 Sir Humphrey Gilbert

11 François Rabelais – hence Rabelaisian

12 Robert Dudley, Earl of Leicester

13 Ivan the Terrible

14 Phillip II, in 1554

15 Giorgio Vasari

16 Amritsar, site of the Golden Temple

17 Hans Holbein, the Younger

18 Cyprus

19 Jacques Cartier

20 Ben Jonson, in 1598

1   Which 1504 masterpiece made Michelangelo famous across Italy?

2   What is the alternative name for Leonardo's *Mona Lisa*?

3   What sank off Southsea on 19 July 1545?

4   Which Italian painter's name means 'little dyer'?

5   Who commanded the English fleet that defeated the Spanish Armada?

6   Which of Henry VIII's wives was the mother of Edward VI?

7   What was the capital of the Inca empire, captured by Pizarro?

8   Which cousin did Elizabeth I have executed?

9   What was Shakespeare's star sign?

10 Which two European countries united between 1536 and 1543 with one official language and one body of law?

11 Which Italian dramatic genre featured Scaramouche and Pantalone?

12 Which Portuguese explorer discovered Brazil?

13 What name was given to the members of guilds of poets and singers of whom the most famous were Hans Sachs and Hans Folz?

14 Who was made Archbishop of Canterbury under Henry VII but burned at the stake as a heretic under Queen Mary?

15 Which Renaissance architect, born at Padua in 1508, developed a style that became the basis of much of English Georgian architecture in the 18th century?

16 Which Lord Chancellor did Henry VIII sack after the Pope refused to annul his marriage?

17 What is the name of Michelangelo's mural behind the altar in the Sistine Chapel?

18 Which French king founded the Bourbon dynasty?

19 What has a dome by Michelangelo (and a 17th-century colonnade by Bernini)?

20 Which writer lost a hand at the battle of Lepanto?

16th Century

1   *His giant statue of David in Florence*

2   *La Gioconda*

3   *The Mary Rose*

4   *Tintoretto*

5   *Lord Howard of Effingham, Lord High Admiral of the English Navy*

6   *Jane Seymour*

7   *Cuzco*

8   *Mary, Queen of Scots*

9   *Taurus*

10   *England and Wales*

11   *Commedia dell'arte*

12   *Pedro Alvares Cabral in 1500*

13   *Meistersingers*

14   *Thomas Cranmer*

15   *Andrea Palladio – hence Palladian*

16   *Thomas Wolsey*

17   *The Last Judgement*

18   *Henry IV*

19   *St Peter's in Rome*

20   *Cervantes*

1 Who was made physician to Charles IX of France after predicting how Henry II would die?

2 What did financier Thomas Gresham say in the maxim known as 'Gresham's law'?

3 How did the last Inca emperor Atahualpa die?

4 What is the Latin term for the common potato?

5 Which line follows: 'But soft, what light through yonder window breaks?'?

6 What was the Flemish doctor Andreas Vesalius the first to do?

7 Who studied at Cracow and Bologna and wrote *On the Revolutions of the Holy Spheres*?

8 Who were the five sovereigns of the House of Tudor?

9 The title of which famous book comes from Greek words meaning 'nowhere'?

10 Which order of monks gives its name to a hot drink?

11 Who tames Shakespeare's shrew?

12 Which Jesuit was known as the Apostle of the Indies?

13 Which tsar became the subject of a play by Pushkin and an opera by Mussorgsky?

14 What is the name of the 1530 document that defined the creed of the Lutheran church?

15 Who sailed to the West Indies with Sir Francis Drake and was knighted for helping defeat the Spanish Armada?

16 Who provided a safe haven for Martin Luther when he was excommunicated and outlawed?

17 Who were the two painter sons of the painter Pieter Brueghel the Elder?

18 Which Dutch philosopher wrote the international best seller *The Praise of Folly*?

19 Who was Aztec emperor when the conquistador Cortes invaded Mexico?

20 Which Ottoman sultan was known as the 'Magnificent'?

1   *Nostradamus*

2   *That bad money tends to drive out good*

3   *He was sentenced to death by strangulation by the conquistadores in 1533*

4   Solanum tuberosum

5   *'It is the east and Juliet is the sun'*

6   *Dissect the human body*

7   *Nicolaus Copernicus*

8   *Henry VII (1485–1509), Henry VIII (1509–47), Edward VI (1546–53), Mary I (1553–58), Elizabeth I (1558-1603)*

9   *Utopia, by Thomas More*

10   *Capuchin monks – hence cappuccino*

11   *Petruchio*

12   *St Francis Xavier*

13   *Boris Godunov*

14   *Augsburg Confession*

15   *Sir Martin Frobisher*

16   *The Elector of Saxony*

17   *Pieter the Younger and Jan*

18   *Desiderius Erasmus*

19   *Montezuma II*

20   *Suleiman I*

Century 15th

1   What were the names of the ships used in Christopher Columbus's first voyage to the New World?

2   Who built the dome of Florence cathedral?

3   In which town was Joan of Arc burned at the stake?

4   William Caxton set up his first printing press in the Flemish town of Bruges. What took him to Bruges in the first place?

5   In which Florentine gallery is Botticelli's *The Birth of Venus*?

6   Which friar threw the Medicis out of Florence to set up a democratic republic?

7   Who was the most famous student of Andrea del Verrocchio?

8   Which Portuguese explorer was the first European to sail around the southern tip of Africa to India?

9   Where would a woman have worn a hennin?

10   Where was the last stronghold of the Moors in Spain?

11   Who allegedly had a child with her father the Pope?

12   Who were the two little princes killed in the Bloody Tower at the Tower of London?

13   Which king founded Eton College as a grammar school in 1440?

14   How did Venezuela get its name?

15   Which royal marriage united the warring houses of York and Lancaster?

16   In which Spanish gallery does Hieronymus Bosch's masterpiece *The Garden of Earthly Delights* hang?

17   Which conflict lasted from 1337 to 1453?

18   Which city, now the capital of Burkina Faso, was the capital of the Mossi empire from the 15th century?

19   Which Italian painter, who died in 1492, is said to have been among the first to apply a scientific method to perspective?

20   What nationality was Henry the Navigator?

1   Santa Maria, Pinta *and* Nina

2   *Filippo Brunelleschi*

3   *Rouen, in 1431*

4   *He was a wool merchant*

5   *The Uffizi Gallery*

6   *Girolamo Savonarola*

7   *Leonardo da Vinci*

8   *Vasco da Gama*

9   *On her head. It was a pointed 'steeple' cap with a veil*

10 *Granada*

11 *Lucrezia Borgia*

12 *Edward V and Richard, Duke of York*

13 *Henry VI*

14 *European explorers named it Venezuela or 'Little Venice' because the coastal Indians lived in houses on stilts*

15 *Henry VII and Elizabeth of York*

16 *The Prado in Madrid*

17 *The Hundred Years War*

18 *Ouagadougou*

19 *Piero della Francesca*

20 *Portuguese*

1   Which king won the Battle of Agincourt?

2   On which famous object would you find the words 'Cormac McCarthy fortis me fieri facit'?

3   Which pope founded the Spanish Inquisition?

4   Which term do Italians use to refer to the 15th century and the early Renaissance?

5   What was the eldest son of a French king called?

6   What did the Scottish parliament ban in 1457 because it interfered with archery practise?

7   Which style of architecture does King's College Chapel, Cambridge, epitomise?

8   Which Italian explorer became the first European to reach the mainland of North America while commanding an expedition for Henry VII?

9   What type of cavalry originated in Hungary and was taken up by most European armies?

10   Who founded the Sikh religion?

11   Which was the first battle of the Wars of the Roses?

12   In which city were most French kings crowned?

13   Who wrote the prose romance *Le Morte d'Arthur*?

14   Who led 30,000 heavily armed Kentishmen in an occupation of London against Henry VI?

15   What was the language of the Incas?

16   Who defeated whom at Bosworth, the last battle of the Wars of the Roses?

17   Who was drowned in a butt of malmsey wine?

18   What nationality was the painter Hieronymus Bosch?

19   Which Medici was known as 'the Magnificent'?

20   Which marriage united the kingdoms of Castille and Aragon?

1   Henry V

2   The Blarney Stone ('Cormac McCarthy had me built strong')

3   Pope Sixtus IV

4   Quattrocento

5   A dauphin

6   Golf

7   Perpendicular

8   John Cabot, who got to Cape Breton Island in 1497

9   Hussars

10 Guru Nanak

11 Battle of St Albans, in 1455

12 Reims

13 Thomas Malory

14 Jack Cade in Cade's Rebellion

15 Quechua

16 Henry of Richmond, the future Henry VII, defeated Richard III

17 George, Duke of Clarence, for plotting against his brother Edward IV

18 Dutch

19 Lorenzo

20 Ferdinand and Isabella's

1 How many times did Christopher Columbus cross the Atlantic?

2 Which was the first book to be printed in English?

3 Which monk was the first Inquisitor General of the Spanish Inquisition?

4 Which nationalist defeated Henry IV three times in two years?

5 Which was the first town liberated by Joan of Arc in her bid to expel the English from France?

6 What is the name of the Inca city perched on 1000-foot-high cliffs discovered in 1911?

7 Who was the first monarch of the House of Lancaster?

8 Who was Queen Mab, according to English and Welsh legend?

9 Who was the first European to use printing from moveable type?

10 Who was the first person to be buried in Poet's Corner?

11 After whom was America named?

12 What was Botticelli's first name?

13 What did Sir Bors, Sir Perceval and Sir Galahad have in common in Thomas Malory's romance *Le Morte D'Arthur*?

14 Which Italian painter became a monk and was tried for abducting a nun?

15 In whose reign did the Wars of the Roses break out?

16 Which king did Joan of Arc help on to the throne?

17 Which Dutch brothers are said to have originated the modern process of oil painting?

18 Who was known as the 'Kingmaker'?

19 What was the name of Europe's first mental hospital?

20 Which German painter and master engraver produced the first-known self-portrait in European art?

1   *Eight times in four voyages to the New World*

2   *History of Troy, printed by William Caxton*

3   *Torquemada*

4   *Owen Glendower*

5   *Orléans*

6   *Machu Picchu*

7   *Henry IV (1399–1413)*

8   *The queen of the fairies*

9   *Johannes Gutenberg*

10 *Geoffrey Chaucer*

11 *The Florentine navigator Amerigo Vespucci*

12 *Sandro (Alessandro)*

13 *They were the only three knights to see the Holy Grail uncovered*

14 *Fra Filippo Lippi*

15 *Henry VI*

16 *Charles VII of France*

17 *Jan and Hubert van Eyck*

18 *Richard Neville, Earl of Warwick*

19 *St Mary of Bethlehem or 'Bedlam'*

20 *Albrecht Dürer*

1 Who defeated Edward II at Bannockburn?

2 Who met up at the Tabard Inn before a long journey?

3 Who invaded Persia, occupied Moscow for a year, sacked Baghdad and built pyramids of his victims' skulls?

4 Who revolted in 1381?

5 In which abbey are Robert the Bruce and many other Scottish kings buried?

6 Where would you find the words 'honi soit qui mal y pense' inscribed?

7 Which cathedral is Europe's longest medieval church?

8 Which public office with no responsibilities and normally held by a cabinet member was created in the middle of the 14th century?

9 At which 1346 battle did English bowmen prove superior to French cavalry?

10 In which city did the poor Ciompi wool workers revolt against the power of the guilds?

11 Where did Edward II's death by red-hot-poker take place?

12 Which queen united Norway, Denmark and Sweden?

13 What was Ockham's razor?

14 Which order ruled Rhodes in the 14th century?

15 Who was the first Scottish king of the House of Stuart?

16 What name is given to reformer John Wycliffe's followers, many of whom were burned at the stake?

17 Who wrote the *Divine Comedy*?

18 Who was the last Plantagenet king?

19 Which empire lasted from 1300 until the 20th century?

20 Who was born in Caernarvon Castle and became the first English Prince of Wales?

14th Century

1 Robert the Bruce

2 The pilgrims in The Canterbury Tales

3 Tamerlane

4 The English peasants, in the Peasants' Revolt

5 Dunfermline Abbey

6 On the garter of the Order of the Garter, founded by Edward III

7 Winchester Cathedral

8 The chancellor of the duchy of Lancaster

9 Battle of Crécy

10 Florence

11 Berkeley Castle

12 Queen Margaret of Denmark, Norway and Sweden, by the Union of Kalmar (1397)

13 A principle in philosophy by William of Ockham that one should assume as little as possible

14 Knights Hospitallers

15 Robert II (1371–90)

16 Lollards

17 Dante

18 Richard II (1377–99)

19 The Ottoman Empire

20 Edward (later King Edward II), son of Edward I

1 Which king of England sparked off the Hundred Years War by claiming the French throne?

2 What did *Yersinia pestis* cause across Europe?

3 What kind of religious painting was the Russian Andrei Rublev a master of?

4 How many husbands did the Wife of Bath have?

5 What was the capital of Mongol ruler Tamerlane's empire?

6 Around the main square of which Italian city has the Palio horse race been run regularly since the Middle Ages?

7 Which empire lost China in 1368?

8 Which Peasants' Revolt leader popularised the slogan: 'When Adam delved and Eve span/ Who was then the gentleman?'

9 Where were Popes based for most of the 14th century?

10 In which medieval poem does a beheaded knight vow to behead his beheader?

11 Which major school of Italian painting did Duccio di Buoninsegna help to found?

12 Which hated levy was one of the main causes of the Peasants' Revolt?

13 Which English reformer said: 'I am always glad to explain my faith to anyone, and above all to the Bishop of Rome'?

14 What is an alternative term for a miracle play?

15 Which battle against France in 1340 constituted England's first major naval victory?

16 What name is given to the verse style – based around accents on syllables – revived in the 14th century in such poems as *Piers Plowman* and *Sir Gawain and the Green Knight*?

17 Which son of King Edward III was born in Ghent in 1340?

18 What name is given to the trading confederation that included more than 150 north European towns in the 14th century?

19 Which classic story about a Trojan prince who falls in love did Geoffrey Chaucer turn into an 8,239-line poem?

20 Which royal dynasty did Philip VI establish in France in 1328?

1   *Edward III, in 1337*

2   *The Black Death*

3   *Icon painting*

4   *Five*

5   *Samarkand*

6   *Siena*

7   *Mongol Empire*

8   *John Ball*

9   *Avignon*

10   *Sir Gawain and the Green Knight*

11   *The Sienese School*

12   *An exorbitant poll tax*

13   *John Wycliffe*

14   *A mystery play*

15   *Battle of Sluys*

16   *Alliterative*

17   *John of Gaunt*

18   *Hanseatic League*

19   Troilus and Criseyde

20   *House of Valois*

1 In which Canterbury Tale is Nicholas's backside scorched by a love rival?

2 How did Wat Tyler die?

3 How long did it take the Black Death to travel from England to Scotland?

4 Which Italian praised the unobtainable Laura in many of his poems?

5 Which Austrian tyrant did William Tell shoot?

6 At which 1389 battle did the Turks defeat the Serbs to take control of most of the Balkans?

7 Which young prince won his spurs at the Battle of Crécy?

8 Who designed the red, white and green marble bell tower of Florence cathedral?

9 Who founded the Ottoman Empire?

10 To which author, of whom little is known, is the Middle English poem *Piers Plowman* attributed?

11 Who founded the Ming dynasty in China?

12 Who became king of England after leading a revolt against Richard II?

13 What proportion of Europe's population died from the Black Death?

14 What name is given to the dispute of 1378 to 1417 in which rival popes had seats in Italy and France?

15 Which Gascon knight was the favourite of Edward II?

16 Which mistress of Edward III is said to have stripped his corpse of all its jewellery?

17 Who headed England's government until the boy-king Richard II came of age?

18 What was the nickname of Philip IV of France, who ordered the torture and execution of the Knights Templar?

19 Which school in the south of England did William of Wykeham found?

20 In whose reign did Geoffrey Chaucer complete *The Canterbury Tales*?

Century 14th

1 The Miller's Tale

2 *He was stabbed to death by the Lord Mayor of London*

3 *Two years*

4 *Petrarch*

5 *Gessler*

6 *Battle of Kosovo*

7 *Edward the Black Prince*

8 *Giotto*

9 *Osman I*

10 *William Langland*

11 *Chu Yüan-chang, in 1368*

12 *Henry IV (Bolingbroke), in 1399*

13 *About one third*

14 *The Great Schism*

15 *Piers Gaveston*

16 *Alice Perrers*

17 *John of Gaunt*

18 *Philip the Fair*

19 *Winchester*

20 *Richard II's*

1   Which emperor did Marco Polo serve for nearly 20 years?

2   What was the poet Dante's surname?

3   Which other country did Edward I of England declare himself king of in 1296?

4   What was unusual about the Crusade of 1212?

5   In which style of Gothic is Salisbury cathedral built?

6   What were the supposed four humors – or liquids – of the body in medieval times?

7   Which stone did Edward I capture in 1296 and bring to London?

8   Whose empire on his death in 1227 stretched from China to the edge of Europe?

9   Which north west African kingdom, founded in the 13th century, is famous for its bronze sculptures, carved ivories and other artworks?

10   Which Italian philosopher and theologian was known as 'Doctor Angelicus'?

11   The northern stretch of which thousand-mile canal was built at the end of the 13th century?

12   With which subject is Leonardo Fibonacci associated?

13   Which female follower of St Francis was proclaimed patron saint of television because she saw a mass from a great distance?

14   Which French poem was begun by Guillaume de Lorris and finished by Jean de Meung?

15   Who led Russian forces to victory over the Teutonic Knights on frozen Lake Peipus in 1242?

16   Which army terrorised Europe under Batu Khan, grandson of Genghis?

17   Which language is derived from medieval German but written in an ancient non-European script?

18   Which Holy Grail epic by Wolfram von Eschenbach was turned into an opera by Wagner?

19   Which Scottish queen was called the Maid of Norway?

20   What were the barons who controlled troubled frontier regions between England and Wales called?

1 Kublai Khan

2 Alighieri

3 Scotland

4 It was the Children's Crusade

5 Early English

6 Blood, phlegm, yellow bile and black bile

7 The Stone of Scone – or Destiny – on which Scottish kings were crowned

8 Genghis Khan's

9 Benin

10 St Thomas Aquinas

11 The Grand Canal in China

12 Mathematics

13 St Clare of Assisi

14 Romance of the Rose

15 Alexander Nevsky

16 The Golden Horde

17 Yiddish, written in Hebrew

18 Parzifal

19 Queen Margaret, daughter of Eric II, king of Norway

20 Marcher Lords

1   At which meadow did King John put his seal to Magna Carta?

2   Which country was excommunicated by Pope Innocent III in 1208?

3   In which country did the sonnet originate?

4   What was Marco Polo's home town?

5   What is the name of the map drawn by David de Bello at Hereford Cathedral showing Jerusalem at the centre of the world?

6   What name is given to the Parliament summoned by Edward I in 1295 that was the first to admit members who were not aristocrats or clerics?

7   How many major Crusades were there between 1095 and 1270?

8   What was the name – meaning 'loaf-mass' – of the medieval harvest festival celebrated on August 1?

9   Which former slaves sat on the Egyptian throne for hundreds of years?

10   What does 'Genghis Khan' mean?

11   Which heretical sect was the focus of Pope Lucius III's crusade of 1208?

12   Which 13th-century English philosopher and scientist predicted the widespread use of gunpowder, mechanized ships, the automobile and the airplane?

13   Who was king of England from the age of nine until the age of 65?

14   Which archbishop of Canterbury led the barons in their struggle with King John and was the architect of Magna Carta?

15   What was the capital of the Mali kingdom?

16   Which countries formed the 'Auld Alliance' in 1295?

17   Who was the legendary Christian king supposed in medieval times to govern a powerful empire in Ethiopia?

18   What does 'Magna Carta' mean?

19   Which UK-administered island was Norwegian until 1266 when it was ceded to Scotland?

20   Which citadel in southern Spain has an Arabic name meaning 'red fort'?

13th *Century*

1   Runnymede

2   England

3   Italy

4   Venice

5   Mappa Mundi

6   The Model Parliament

7   Eight

8   Lammas

9   The Mamelukes

10 Mighty ruler

11 Albigenses, or Cathars, of southern France

12 Roger Bacon

13 Henry III (1216–72)

14 Stephen Langton

15 Timbuktu

16 Scotland and France

17 Prester John

18 The great charter

19 Isle of Man

20 The Alhambra

1   What did the Japanese dub the hurricane that wrecked Kublai Khan's army when he tried to invade in 1281?

2   Which three people does Dante place in the lowest ring of hell in his Inferno?

3   What did the Lateran Council of 1215 order Christians to do at least once a year?

4   Which collection of Goliardic verse did Carl Orff set to music in the 20th century?

5   Which city, which has been the capital of two large empires, was captured and ransacked by the army of the Fourth Crusade?

6   Which family took over Monaco at the end of the 13th century?

7   Which worldwide order of friars, also known as Black Friars, was founded in France in 1215?

8   Which Welsh prince was formally recognised by Henry III of England as Prince of Wales?

9   Which north west African empire flourished for over 800 years until much of its was taken over by the Mali empire in the 13th century?

10   Which 13th-century German singer did Wagner write an opera about?

11   Which nationalist took the title 'Governor of Scotland' after defeating the English at Stirling Bridge?

12   Who summoned the first English parliament to give representation to the towns?

13   Which Mongol emperor founded the Yuan dynasty in China, based his court at Peking and extended his empire to Indo-China?

14   From the name of which Scottish monk is the word 'dunce' derived?

15   Which king was imprisoned by Simon de Montfort?

16   Which cathedral in north England is renowned for its stained glass, especially the 'Five Sisters' window?

17   Which landlocked European country was placed under the joint rule of France and Spain in 1278?

18   Which Holy Roman Emperor won back Jerusalem in the Sixth Crusade?

19   Which is the oldest Oxford college?

20   Which Turkish empire preceded the Ottoman Empire?

13th Century

1 *Kamikaze – 'the divine wind'*

2 *Brutus, Cassius and Judas Iscariot*

3 *Confess to a priest*

4 Carmina Burana

5 *Constantinople, in 1204*

6 *The Grimaldis*

7 *Dominicans, by St Dominic*

8 *Llewelyn II*

9 *The Ghana empire*

10 *Tannhäuser*

11 *William Wallace*

12 *Simon de Montfort, in 1265*

13 *Kublai Khan*

14 *John Duns Scotus*

15 *Henry III*

16 *York Minster*

17 Andorra

18 *Frederick II*

19 *University College, founded in 1249*

20 *Seljuk Empire*

1. Who commanded the Muslim forces that captured Jerusalem in 1187?

2. Who were the first three Plantagenet kings?

3. Which French poet wrote some of the first stories about King Arthur, including *Lancelot, or the Knight of the Cart*?

4. King Henry I died of a surfeit of which fish?

5. Which English king spent just six months of his 10-year reign in England?

6. What was the nickname of the hirsute Holy Roman Emperor Frederick I?

7. What relation was Richard I to William the Conqueror?

8. Who was Henry II's mistress, poisoned by his wife Eleanor of Acquitaine?

9. What was the nickname of Henry, Duke of Saxony, the husband of Matilda, daughter of Henry II of England?

10. Where is the great 12th-century temple of Angkor Wat?

11. What is the origin of the word Plantagenet?

12. Which university was founded first – Oxford or Cambridge?

13. Which heir to the throne did Henry I lock up for nearly 30 years?

14. Which historical record, begun under King Alfred, still had entries in the 12th century?

15. Where was Thomas à Becket murdered by four knights?

16. Which organisation of knights, founded in Palestine in 1190, later controlled Prussia?

17. What were the seven 'Liberal Arts' in the Middle Ages?

18. Who was the only queen of England never to set foot in the realm?

19. Which originally nomadic people occupied north China in 1127?

20. Who drowned in the 'White Ship'?

Century 12th

1 Saladin

2 Henry II (1154–89), Richard I (1189–99) and King John (1199–1216)

3 Chrétien de Troyes

4 Lampreys

5 Richard (I) the Lionheart

6 Barbarossa or Redbeard

7 Great-great-grandson

8 Fair Rosamund

9 Henry the Lion

10 Cambodia

11 From 'planta genista', a sprig of broom, which was the emblem of the Plantagenets

12 Oxford, traditionally said to have been founded in the mid-12th century

13 His elder brother Robert, son of William the Conquerer

14 The Anglo Saxon Chronicle

15 In front of the altar of Canterbury Cathedral

16 Knights of the Teutonic Order

17 Arithmetic, geometry, music, astronomy, grammar, rhetoric and logic

18 Queen Berengaria of Navarre, wife of Richard I

19 The Manchurians

20 Henry I's only son, William, and daughter Adela

12th Century

1   Who was Richard I's faithful minstrel?

2   Who was the only English pope?

3   Which faith did Stephen Nemanya I encourage the Serbs to adopt?

4   What name is given to the light Latin verse made up by the students, wandering clerics and minstrels of medieval Germany, France and England?

5   Who was nicknamed Lackland?

6   Which order was founded in about 1118 to guard the route of pilgrims to Jerusalem?

7   Which famous rabbi and scholar was born in Spain in 1135?

8   Which preacher and future saint drew pilgrims in their droves to the Cistercian monastery at Clairvaux?

9   What were Guelfs and Ghibelines?

10   Of which country did Saladin become sultan in 1135?

11   To whom was Eleanor of Aquitaine married before she tied the knot with Henry II of England?

12   Which London hospital was founded in 1123?

13   The Church of Saint Denis outside Paris is said to be the first example of which architectural style?

14   What is Ghen Guei said to have invented in China?

15   Which part of France did Henry I unite with England?

16   What name is given to the German lyric poets of the 12th and 13th centuries who sang about love?

17   What was Thomas à Becket's position before he became Archbishop of Canterbury?

18   Why are Henry II and Richard I known as 'Angevin' kings?

19   What was the nickname of Louis VI of France?

20   Which country defeated the Muslims to become an independent kingdom under Afonso I?

1   Blondel

2   Nicholas Breakspear or Adrian IV (1154–9)

3   The Greek Orthodox

4   Goliardic verse

5   King John

6   Knights Templars

7   Moses Maimonides

8   St Bernard

9   Rival political parties in Germany and later Italy

10 Egypt

11 King Louis VII of France

12 Bart's

13 Gothic

14 Gunpowder

15 Normandy

16 Minnesingers

17 Chancellor

18 Henry II, father of Richard I, was Count of Anjou in France before he took the throne of England

19 The Fat

20 Portugal

1   Which king set up the Curia Regis, the forerunner of the civil service?

2   Which daughter of Henry I invaded England after her cousin Stephen seized the throne?

3   What are the ingredients of gunpowder?

4   Which religious movement entered Japan from China in the 12th century?

5   Which philosopher's affair with a student sparked a medieval scandal?

6   Who captured Richard the Lionheart and passed him to the Emperor of Germany, who kept him in a tower for ransom?

7   What is the origin of the word 'exchequer'?

8   During whose reign did the English conquest of Ireland start?

9   Which port, now in modern Israel, was captured by the Crusaders in 1104, lost to Saladin in 1187 and won back by Richard the Lionheart four years later?

10   What title did Minamoto Yoritomo assume in 1185, the first in Japanese history?

11   Which major Crusader fortress (now in Syria) was built in 1142?

12   What did Andrew, Duke of Vladimir, found in 1160?

13   Which city did Muhammed of Ghur take in 1192 to found an Islamic empire?

14   Which Muslim dynasty overthrew the reigning Almoravids in Spain in 1147-9?

15   Which European capital city was captured from the Muslims by an army on its way to the Second Crusade?

16   What did the Concordat of Worms settle?

17   Which monastic order was founded on Mount Carmel in 1155?

18   Who wrote *The History of the Kings of Britain*?

19   Which Byzantine princess wrote the *Alexiad*?

20   What was the alliance of Italian cities which rebelled against the Holy Roman Empire from 1167 to 1183 known as?

12th Century

1   Henry I

2   Matilda (Empress Maud)

3   Saltpetre (potassium nitrate), sulphur and powdered charcoal

4   Zen Buddhism

5   Pierre Abelard, who secretly married Heloise and was castrated on the orders of her uncle

6   Leopold of Austria

7   From the practice of counting out taxes on a chequer board

8   Henry II's

9   Acre

10   Shogun

11   Krak des Chevaliers

12   Moscow

13   Delhi; Muhammed became the first sultan of Delhi

14   The Almohads

15   Lisbon, in 1147

16   The Investiture Controversy between the papacy and the Holy Roman Emperors over the rights of appointing senior clergy

17   The Carmelites

18   Geoffrey of Monmouth, c. 1137

19   Anna Comnena

20   The Lombard League

1   Which battle did Harold II win three weeks before losing the Battle of Hastings?

2   Which is the largest and oldest tower in the Tower of London?

3   Who built the first Westminster Abbey?

4   Which king of England was killed by an arrow while hunting in the New Forest?

5   Which were the original five Cinque ports?

6   What did Byzantine emperor Basil II do with the 15,000 prisoners he took after defeating the Bulgarians in 1014?

7   Where did William the Conqueror land when he invaded England in 1066?

8   Who led a revolt against the Normans from his stronghold on the Isle of Ely?

9   What name was given to the hypothetical substance that alchemists believed would turn base metals into gold?

10   Which Italian town has the oldest university in Europe?

11   What is the knight Roderigo Diaz de Vivar usually called?

12   Which island kingdom did the Normans conquer between 1061 and 1091?

13   Which religious community has barred women and female animals from its land since the 11th century?

14   What was the name of the council of Anglo Saxon kings from which Parliament may be said to have evolved?

15   Which Holy Roman Emperor deposed Pope Gregory VII after being excommunicated twice in four years?

16   Who was king of England in 1000?

17   Under which dynasty did China outperform Europe in many fields of technology in the 11th, 12th and 13th centuries?

18   Which king of Norway became its patron saint?

19   Which Persian doctor's *Canon of Medicine* became a standard text for hundreds of years?

20   Which American people based their capital at Tula, north of present-day Mexico City?

1   The Battle of Stamford Bridge

2   The White Tower, built by William the Conqueror

3   Edward the Confessor

4   William Rufus

5   Sandwich, Dover, Romney, Hythe and Hastings

6   Blinded them all except for a handful who were blinded in one eye only and made to lead the rest home

7   Pevensey, Sussex

8   Hereward the Wake

9   The philosopher's stone

10 Bologna, founded in 1088

11 El Cid

12 Sicily

13 The monastic community at Mount Athos in northern Greece

14 The Witan

15 Henry IV

16 Ethelred the Unready

17 Song, or Sung, dynasty

18 King Olaf II

19 Avicenna's

20 The Toltecs

1 Who looked at Lady Godiva as she rode naked through Coventry?

2 Who discovered America in 1000?

3 Where in London can you see the Domesday Book?

4 What was the Viking-controlled eastern section of England called?

5 Who was the son of Findlaech and, from 1040, king of Scotland?

6 In which style is the church of St Mark in Venice built?

7 Which tax did Ethelred the Unready raise to bribe invaders to stay away?

8 Of which architectural style is Durham cathedral said to be one of the finest examples?

9 Which French dynasty ruled from 987 to 1328?

10 Which cathedral did Archbishop Lanfranc instigate the building of in 1070?

11 Which Italian scholar became Archbishop of Canterbury in 1093?

12 Augsburg Cathedral has the earliest known what?

13 Who said while standing on a beach: 'God is the only king whom all things obey'?

14 Upon whose promise to pass him the crown did William the Conqueror base his claim to the English throne?

15 Which saint established the Byzantine rite of orthodox Christianity as the Russian national faith?

16 The *Ruodlieb*, a poem by a Bavarian monk, contained the first European reference to what kind of dancing?

17 Which minority sect sprang up in 11th-century Egypt believing in the divinity of the Fatimid caliph al-Hakim?

18 What did Pi Sheng invent around 1045?

19 Which Muslim dynasty, claiming to be descended from the prophet Muhammad's daughter, ruled Egypt for 200 years?

20 The poet Firdausi's work *The Book of Kings*, written c.1020 is the national epic of which country?

1   Peeping Tom

2   The Norse explorer Leif Ericsson

3   At the Public Records Office

4   Danelaw

5   Macbeth

6   Byzantine

7   The Danegeld

8   Romanesque (or Norman)

9   Capetians

10   Canterbury

11   St Anselm

12   Stained glass window

13   King Canute when the tide refused his orders

14   His cousin King Edward the Confessor's.

15   Vladimir I, Grand Duke of Kiev

16   Dancing in couples, in 1050

17   The Druse

18   Movable type for printing

19   The Fatimids, who claimed to be decended from Fatima

20   Persia (Iran)